365 days

of

The ~~Year~~ Truth

Written by:

Terence Wallen

DMJ Publishing

365 Days Of The Year Truth

Published in England, UK, by DMJ Publishing

www.dmjpublishing.co.uk

Cover Design: Scale DM

Photography By: Riverstudio for Scale DM

Table of Contents

Foreword

When I think of words spoken by another person (quotes) I no longer think of William Shakespeare, Thomas Edison or Oscar Wilde like I was taught in school. Today I think of great inspirational men and women gone on the journey before me who helped to shape the path, I walk THIS day. Such people as Jim Rohn, Langston Hughes, Steve Jobs, Michelle Obama, Tony Robbins and of course Oprah Winfrey. You and I are now the givers of life's wisdom and hearing others quote #OurTruths.

The world as we know it is changing right before our very eyes, join Terence Wallen as he masterfully prepares you for the day ahead with 365 of truths that inspire, teach, reach, and allow you to reflect on the day ahead and the days gone.

Watching Terence's growth over the many years that I have known him, I believe that this book has been over 20 years in the making. In this book you will see how the very idea of a new day is a beautiful gift waiting to be revealed.

Before you turn the page, and embark on a magical 365-day journey with this book that will forever be your companion, I will leave you with this quote by philospher Ralph Waldo Emerson.

"Finish each day and be done with it. You have done what you could. Some blunders and absurdities no doubt crept in; forget them as soon as you can. Tomorrow is a new day. You shall begin it serenely and with too high a spirit to be encumbered with your old nonsense." **- Ralph Waldo Emerson**

Forward by
Darryl James
Author & Leading Business Strategist

January

January 1

"Your time is limited, so don't waste it living someone else's life."

Steve Jobs

"At the end of the day, I am all I really have, I value time over everything, everything else I can get back, once time is past, that is it. Live your life, it is your gift"

January 2

"If you cannot do great things, do small things in a great way."

Napoleon Hill

"Whatever it is I do; I ensure that quality overrides quantity. Several small great things will eventually amount to several greater things. Do not underestimate your greatness, thou you may not recognise it, others will"

January 3

"I have to let my people close to my heart know what's really going on"

Paul Bradford

"Anything that I deem important, I share with my immediate circle. A problem shared is a problem halved, also sharing your joys and achievements will bring warmth to your circle and inspire others. Your real ones want to be informed and share your journey sincerely"

January 4

"Luck is what happens
when preparation meets opportunity.'

Seneca

"Live life prepared for every eventuality. Prepare yourself daily for anything, good, bad, and indifferent. This preparation be it physical or emotional will place you in a better position when the opportunity comes, and rest assured opportunities will arise, so be ready."

January 5

"Move out of your comfort zone. You can only grow if you are willing to feel awkward and uncomfortable when you try something new."

Brian Tracy

"There is no growth in being comfortable, many a times my greatest success will happen on the back of chaos, vulnerability, and bullshit. I've realised I've learnt and grown best when I've been uncomfortable"

January 6

"One sign of maturity is the ability to be comfortable with people who are not like us"

Virgil A. Kraft

"Many a times, I find myself surrounded by dickhead's but remain me because I know who I am and accept who they are. When you are of a certain alignment you will be able to adapt to any situation or surroundings without standing out, it is a wonderful sign of maturity, one of which will serve you well"

January 7

"My response to every situation is, it is all good because even if it isn't I'm going to make sure it will be"

Unknown

"Positive thinking results in positive outcomes. Life will throw things in your way, don't let them stop you, use them to build or use them as stepping stones, either way make good of every bad situation, you either win or you learn, losing is not an option"

January 8

"Every single one of us leaves a legacy.
We influence people every day by what we say and do, what we write, create and share, and all of that influence adds up.
May we use the power of our lives for the good of those we touch"

Unknown

"Remember someone is always watching, for that reason I am always the best version of me. Everyday, every interaction, every act of kindness, everything we do will form part of our legacy, so make sure your actions speak positive volumes now so it will be amplified as part of your legacy in the future"

January 9

"Determine to live life with flair and laughter."

Maya Angelou

"I am always laughing. I am always smiling. I am always dancing. It will be written somewhere 'this person lived their life to the fullest and some more'. Be the firework in the night skies, dimming your light serves no purpose"

January 10

"The only thing worse than being blind is having sight but no vision."

Helen Keller

"You must be able to look beyond what you can initially see, not everything is as it appears, some things require your deeper sense of vision. Tap into those senses and abilities you already have, use them and watch the difference it will make to your life"

January 11

"Be the person who breaks the cycle. If you were judged, choose understanding. If you were rejected, choose acceptance. If you were shamed, choose compassion. Be the person you needed when you were hurting, not the person who hurt you. Vow to be better than what broke you—to heal instead of becoming bitter so you can act from your heart, not your pain"

Lori Deschene

"I have been through all hell and back, well so it seemed at the time. My pains could not break me, so instead I used my heart to make me. I knew I had to make a difference once I established that I through the pain I could show strength, through the lows I could show highs, through the hate I could show love and through it all I could show survival"

January 12

"May your circle decreased in size but increased in value"

Unknown

"It must be quality over quantity with the people you allow within your energy. Do not be fooled by the crowd that cheer you on when your winning but boo you once you have lost. People have a way of sticking around once they realise they can benefit from you, but disappear when the benefits stop. With all my popularity, I removed myself from all persons toxic, irrelevant, negative, bad minded, grudgeful and fake. I am now left with 6 people in my circle and that completes me. Isn't that some shit!!!"

January 13

"A mistake that makes you humble is much better than an achievement that makes you arrogant."

Unknown

"Believe you me, I am full of perfect imperfections. All of which have humbled me, truth be told arrogances would have never got me this far nor would it be accepted by my peeps. We live and we learn, and our flaws once accepted can never be used against us. All achievements are accepted with humbleness and gratitude of which maketh the man"

January 14

"Make efforts to hold yourself to a high standard, and to develop a strong sense of character throughout your life."

Unknown

"Throughout my life I have not and will not drop my standard to entertain those who refuse to raise theirs. I have enough shoulders to stand on of those who came before me so I stand tall with a character to match. Let them who wish to be in your presence raise their game, never lower yours, it will be a long way back up"

January 15

"I got trust issues because people got lying issues"

Unknown

"Yes, I have insecurities, that is because some raaas people to raaas lie. I would rather be hurt with the truth then comforted with a lie. My issues go when you and your behaviour goes"

January 16

"From today start making healthy choices. Not choices that are only healthy for your body, but healthy for your mind. Mind your mind. Mental health is real, please take care of yours"

Terence Wallen

"Feed your mind with the best foods available to you. If I consume shit, it will mess with my mental output which will only = shit. So my friends remember be careful what you input as it will also become your output"

January 17

"Imagine finding both love &
friendship in one person."

Unknown

"I have…. but in multiple baby mothers lol! Now that is a win win situation for me but never everyone is so fortunate as me to have such beautiful ex partners in their life. For you id say find that person of whom you can speak to their heart and their soul and vice versa. Its a different, unexplainable place of comfort if you find both the abundance of love and true friendship in one person"

January 18

"Understand that even an 'understanding heart' grows tired of being understanding and never understood."

Aaliyah Jay

"There are times I give so much of myself and absolutely nothing to myself. With my complexity I have the ability to understand, though my complexities at times make it hard to be understood. Make time for yourself, an empty you can't fill anyone else. Find the balance between giving and being refilled, forever understanding of others but rarely understood"

January 19

"I see you. I'm there too. We're in this together."

Unknown

"Whatever is happening right now in my life, someone somewhere has either been through it or is going through it. There is comfort in knowing I am not alone, and I hope you feel comforted knowing your also not alone. Draw on the experience of others and let it support your journey"

January 20

"Learn the art of patience. Apply discipline to your thoughts. Impatience breeds anxiety, fear, discouragement, and failure. Patience creates confidence, decisiveness, and a rational outlook, which eventually leads to success"

Brian Adams

"My mother would say 'A patient man rides a donkey'. It's not about the journey, it is about reaching the destination. There is no shortcut to greatness. The journey is the best bit and the destination is the reward, so no matter how long it takes just don't give up"

January 21

"Anyone who thinks sitting in church can make you a Christian must also think that sitting in a garage can make you a car"

Garrison Keillor

"I am what I am regardless of the environment. If I were a product of my environment, who knows what I would be. I'm destined to make my environment a product of me, so I invest greatly into the people and places from where I came. Its less about where you are and more about who you are"

January 22

"Moving on does not mean you forget about things. It just means you have to accept what happened and continue living."

Erza Scarlet

"Though I may forgive, I will not forget, and I certainly will not carry the weight or burden of any flaws be it mine or yours. Life goes on regardless; the world does not stop because we did"

January 23

"If I had eight hours to chop down a tree, I'd spend six hours sharpening my axe"

Abraham Lincoln

"We must break the cycle, many of those before us worked tirelessly and never really lived, to live and have a life are two different things. The volume of their tremendous work did not equal to a tremendous life, unfortunately nor did they have the rewards to show for it because all their time and energy was consumed in the graft and living was secondary. Work smart not hard, my working day consistent of 4 hours, the other 20 I spend living"

January 24

"Losing someone you love is one of the biggest tests in life. You'll have to carry on without the one you thought you could never live without. Allow yourself time to grieve. The pain & heartache will serve as reminders. Submit to the Almighty's Decree. He will grant you ease"

Mufti Menk

"Fortunately, I have people and I have myself. Everything I have learnt from my loses has allowed me to gain. I have learnt stuff I would have never been taught had the teacher still been here"

January 25

"A lion does not concern himself with the opinions of a sheep. Expecting the world to treat you fairly because you're a good person is like expecting a bull not to attack you because you're a vegetarian".

Tywin Lannister

"I know who I am but not everyone else does and I am cool with that, because I expect nothing, I am never disappointed. I've accepted they will come for me regardless, I've also accepted that regardless of them coming I refuse to be defeated"

January 26

"To attract better, you have to become better. You can't do the same things and expect change. Transform your mindset. Upgrade your habits. Think positive. Be hopeful and consistent with your evolution. It all starts with you and how you feel about yourself"

Unknown

"What I put out is what I get back, I am my circle. Change comes with doing things differently. If you are going to remain the same you may as well be dead. You cant expect change if your doing the same thing over and over again, if you require a different result then you have to change"

January 27

"Winners win on purpose"

Unknown

"I do it because that is all I know. I do it because that is all I can do. Its not by chance, it is by choice. Think like a winner, know you've won before the race, speak success into existence, tell it to the universe and it will be yours. Except nothing else but knowing your already a winner and use this book to prop up your mind, see you on the podium"

January 28

"I am not a product of my circumstances. I am a product of my decisions"

Stephen Covey

"What I am today was born of the decisions I made yesterday be them good or bad. I accept my journey and know my of destination. No regrets, let your greatness come through struggle, turmoil, pain, suffering and the ability to know that this too had to pass"

January 29

"The real measure of our wealth is how much we'd be worth if we lost all our money."

Jowett

"What would i really be worth to everyone if i had nothing tangible to offer? Way more than my net worth. The value in me as a person can only be described as the wealth of input, love, laughter i share with the people i meet. I genuinely believe my measure of wealth as a person would easily out do any amount of money. I feel loved for me not for what i have"

January 30

"There can be no keener revelation of a society's soul than the way in which it treats its children."

Nelson Mandela

"I had faith in every lost soul I ever came across. Some are lost, some found themselves, either way it is our duty to nurture, love, empower and support the younger generations. Let us put into place now that of which will benefit generations to come and they will in turn develop it for future generations after them and so on and so on. We owe it to the children as many of our lessons and teachings came through them"

January 31

"Fear is a manipulative emotion that can trick us into living a boring life"

Donald Miller

"Live your life to the fullest, we only have one chance to make the best of this life, fear is about being afraid, when your mind tells you that you are fearful tell it maybe so but your still going to face your fears regardless of the outcomes, and usually the fear is by far much worse than the reality. I'd rather live on the edge than die bored"
#MyTruth

February

February 1

"You wanna fly, you got to give up the shit that weighs you down."

Toni Morrison

"I am a frequent flyer and at times it is just hand luggage. Extra weight and excess baggage will amount to extra charges. Look at your life this way, why pay for what you need not carry. Anyone weighing you down is a burden, lesson the load and travel light"

February 2

"If we permit ourselves to be tempted by narrow self-interest and vain ambition, if we barter our beliefs for short-term advantage, who will listen when we claim to speak for conscience, and who will contend that our words deserve to be heeded? We must speak out on major world issues, courageously, openly and honestly, and in blunt terms of right and wrong. If we yield to blandishments or threats, if we compromise when no honourable compromise is possible, our influence will be sadly diminished and our prestige woefully prejudiced and weakened. Let us not deny our ideals or sacrifice our right to stand as the champions of the poor, the ignorant, the oppressed everywhere. The acts by which we live and the attitudes by which we act must be clear beyond question. Principles alone can endow our deeds with force and meaning. Let us be true to what we believe that our beliefs may serve and honour us"

H.I.M. Haile Selassie I

"He has spoken, stand up and be counted, refuse to be silenced, speak your truth, not everyone will like it but who cares just as long as you do as to why you chose to be vocal and visual in the first place".

February 3

"Sometimes...
The issue is simply that their ceiling is your floor"

Unknown

"Haters…. I have been there, done that, bought the T-Shirt factory!
What you're now picking up, I've already put down, Its pointless trying to derail me as I passed your station way before you realised you had a grievance. Listen: Just let winners be, the energies they use trying to put others down can be better used in building themselves. Once they accept your walking on their ceiling, they too can start shopping for new shoes and start learning to stride"

February 4

"Maturity is learning to walk away from people and situations that threaten your peace of mind, self-respect, values, morals or self-worth."

Unknown

"I do not entertain foolish and I certainly do not mix with clowns as I am not part of any circus. Walk away from them, leave them conversating with themselves cos only they can understand their own foolery. If you stand and argue with them it may be difficult for others to identify who is the idiot"

February 5

"I am thankful for all those difficult people in my life, they have shown me exactly who I do not want to be"

Unknown

"Let me just thank all those of no substance… Thank you. Your difficultness has made life easy for others and i. You're a teacher and you didn't even know it. Keep being you so we can show future generations how not to become and maybe then the world will be a better place."

February 6

"Character is a quality that embodies many important traits, such as integrity, courage, perseverance, confidence and wisdom. Unlike your fingerprints that you are born with and can't change, character is something that you create within yourself and must take responsibility for changing".

Unknown

"I care more about my character then my reputation. My character is embedded in me, my reputation is embedded in you. Work on your character as that's the true you, your reputation is none of your business…its theirs"

February 7

"Sometimes you have to stop being scared and just go for it. Either it'll work or it won't. That's life".

Alex Elle

"I live on the edge. That way I will see things other cannot see and will not see unless they too come to the edge to. Don't live in fear, it will consume you and hold you a resident. The world of Freedom of spirit is the best place to dwell, take risks, either you win or you learn but you don't lose"

February 8

"Forgiving someone does not mean that their behaviour was "OK." What it does mean is that we're ready to move on. To release the heavy weight. To shape our own life, on our terms, without any unnecessary burdens".

Dr Suzanne Gelb

"Sometimes you just must accept defeat, they win, you lose if when you know you haven't. However, for a peaceful life hand them the trophy, say 'you've won' and keep it moving. Be prepared to lose the battle knowing you've won the war"

February 9

"Hating people takes too much time. Forgive them, not because they deserve it but because you are on a higher level than they are".

Unknown

"I do not hate anyone, I just dislike people's ways. I still acknowledge their existence, even if it is not at eye level"

February 10

"It is your job to respect your partner. But it is also your partner's job to give you something to respect".

"How can I possibly respect a woman who does not respect herself. Expect nothing of me when you see nothing in yourself. Expect everything of me when you see everything in yourself. You deserve someone who loves themselves before they can love you"

February 11

"To be a father requires patience, love and giving up the 'all about me' attitude."

Catherine Pulsifer

"Ask my children, it hasn't been about me for over 3 decades. However….the next 3 decades will certainly be all about me and they will be paying for it"

February 12

"Make someone happy today. Do a good deed. Be kind, even to a stranger."

Unknown

"Spread goodness, Smile, do whatever it takes. Happiness never decreases by being shared. Watch me spread my blessings far and wide! It's like the wind so it will reach you wherever you are, my purpose of life is to live a life of purpose"

February 13

"Everything that happens to you is a reflection of what you believe about yourself. We cannot outperform our level of self-esteem. We cannot draw to ourselves more than we think we are worth".

Iyanla Vanzant

"Believe you can and you will. Speak it into existent, make it happen. Fill yourself with everything that makes you happy and watch it manifest itself into your very being. You are worthy and you must never forget that or else you invite others to forget it too"

February 14

"If you do not love yourself, you will not attract the love you want. If you are not kind to yourself, others will not be kind to you. Whatever it is that you believe about yourself is what the world, and the people around you, will offer you"

Unknown

"The love that I beam warms everyone within my radius, I am generous by default and get it back 10-fold. I believe that I am great and the people around me offer me an abundance of love and greatness too. This is the glue that holds me together"

February 15

"So many of us invest a fortune making ourselves look good to the world, yet inside we are falling apart. It is time to invest on the inside".

Iyanla Vanzant

"I will never be so focused on building a house that I forget to build a home. We can all fake looking good on the outside but the true you knows how you are on the inside and sooner or later it will reveal itself to all. Work on the inner you and the outer you will take care of itself"

February 16

"It matters not who you love, where you love, why you love, when you love or how you love, it matters only that you love."

John Lennon

"Live and love, love to live. The love we know we deserve is the love we will receive. Know your worth and absorb love in all its glory and whilst you're at it give it back in abundance too. What a beautiful world this would be if only we all just focused primarily on loving each other"

February 17

"Choose happiness, not success, as your life's goal. If you become successful but aren't happy, then what is the point?"

Haemin Sunim

"Happiness is the ultimate goal, with that you can achieve anything. Just to be alive should be enough for us to be happy.

Success can come and go but ensure your real achievement is happiness.

Ensure you are responsible for your own happiness, depend on no one to give it you but if its offered grasp it with both hands. Choose happiness now, dwell not on your past and worry not of the future. Make happy your new way of life, as much as you want to breath you must also strive to be happy"

#MyTruth

February 18

"It is impossible to live without failing at something, unless you live so cautiously that you might as well not have lived at all, in which case you have failed by default."

J. K. Rowling

"I have had to fail to appreciate success, had I not failed success would not feel so rewarding. Do not fear failing, fear not trying at all"

February 19

"It is easier to build strong children than to repair broken men."

Frederick Douglass

"I have invested in the foundations of my children and built a kingdom to house my kings and queens. All had to be done early whilst they were impressionable and the foundations where being laid. Nurture the tree from early as it's much harder to bend its branches once its fully grown"

February 20

“The truth is everyone is going to hurt you. You just got to find the ones worth suffering for”

Bob Marley

“I have been hurt numerous times and it was all worth it. No regrets. I’ve learnt so many lessons from hurt, both as a giver and receiver, had it not been for hurt I could have been by far less of a man. I didn’t mind the hurt because it usually came after love and those time I appreciated…so no regrets”

February 21

"Do not dwell in the past, do not dream of the future, concentrate the mind on the present moment."

Buddha

"Tomorrow is not promised to anyone, I will live in the present but look forward to the future. Now is here for the taking and it's here and now that I'm doing my best and living my best"

February 22

"Do not go where the path may lead, go instead where this no path and leave a trail."

Ralph Waldo Emerson

"I do shit my own way. I would be lost in a crowd hence why I stand alone. On my own path, on my own journey but I am always willing to show people how I did it".

February 23

"The supreme art of war is to subdue the enemy without fighting."

Sun Tzu

"Fighting takes way too much effort, that is why I don't engage in battles when I have already figured out an easy way to win the war. Waste not your energy on pointless battles, they think they are battling with you but truth be told the real battle is with themselves"

February 24

"I alone cannot change the world, but I can cast a stone across the waters to create many ripples"

Mother Teresa

"Over time I have helped numerous individual who in turn rewards me by helping numerous individuals, the point of being a leader is that I create more leaders not that I a mass followers".

February 25

"The two most important days in your life are the day you are born and the day you find out why."

Mark Twain

"I give all of credit to my mother and take any remaining credit for myself when I found myself. You must know your purpose, to exist alone is not enough"

February 26

"When I was 5 years old, my mother always told me that happiness was the key to life. When I went to school, they asked me what I wanted to be when I grew up. I wrote down 'happy'. They told me I didn't understand the assignment, and I told them they didn't understand life."

John Lennon

"Everything my mother ever told me still remains, my happy is her happy and her happy is my happy. No matter what people say to you, stick to your truth. They don't have to understand, and you don't really have to care. Just know that's what's ultimately important to you may not be as important to another"

February 27

"Here's to the crazy ones, the misfits, the rebels, the troublemakers, the round pegs in the square holes … the ones who see things differently — they're not fond of rules … You can quote them, disagree with them, glorify or vilify them, but the only thing you can't do is ignore them because they change things … They push the human race forward, and while some may see them as the crazy ones, we see genius …"

Steve Jobs

"It's okay to be different. Its cool to be the one everyone thinks is different, let them say your odd, your quirky, your weird…. that's fine. Its better to stand out from the crowd than just be part of the crowd. Embrace your own normal. Remember… I am not you"

February 28

"The days you are most uncomfortable are the days you learn the most about yourself"

Mary L Bean

"I learnt so much about myself when I faced my biggest fears and was uncomfortable with losing the nearest. The more i learnt about me the better I became, the calmer I became, I appreciated life more, I was ok with being vulnerable.... the uncomfortable road is where the best of my journey began"#MyTruth

February 29

"Throughout life people will make you mad, disrespect you and treat you bad. Let God deal with the things they do, cause hate in your heart will consume you too."

Will Smith

"Yes, I have had all the above plus the extras. I did two things, left them to the almighty and carried on. Not everything and everyone deserves a reaction, hate is a waste of your good time and energy and so are they"

March

March 1

"There are three things you can do with your life: You can waste it, you can spend it, or you can invest it. The best use of your life is to invest it in something that will last longer than your time on Earth."

Rick Warren

"When I leave this earth, I will leave so much behind that you will actually think I am still here"

March 2

"I have a limited amount of time left on this planet, and I'm not gonna spend it being a watered down version of myself just so people can like me."

Bree Christina

"Having experienced losing someone close to me my perspective on life itself has changed, not only that but I'm placed the greatest value on time, we may stop but time does not, so whilst I'm here I'm going to live the life I love and love the life I live. I care zero who likes me because I'm so focused on those that love me"
#MyTruth

March 3

"Nowhere can man find a quieter or more untroubled retreat than in his own soul."

Marcus Aurelius

"I've embraced Solace and solitude. I love silence, I love peace of mind, I love speaking to myself and saying nothing in meditation. When my silence speaks volumes I know its a conversation worth having"
#MyTruth

March 4

"Try not to confuse attachment with love. Attachment is about fear and dependency, and has more to do with love of self than love of another. Love without attachment is the purest love because it isn›t about what others can give you because you›re empty. It is about what you can give others because you're already full."

Yasmin Mogahed.

"Everyone who has ever been loved by me in whatever shape or form, knows I make it look easy because I'm already filled with an abundance of love to share. I've had women attached for all the wrong reasons and released them for all the right reasons so they too can find love within themselves"
#MyTruth

March 5

"Peace of mind
That's just what I seek to find
I ain't in the mood
I just need some solitude"

Lila Ike

"Simply leave me alone, I'm with myself and I couldn't wish for better company"
#MyTruth

March 6

"If you don't design your own life plan, chances are you'll fall into someone else's plan. And guess what they have planned for you? Not much"

Jim Rohn

"Its every man for themselves, I put me first and I won't allow anyone to use me to get what they want, the place is full of users, I see them all the time, their plan is solely to win so I ensure I don't lose"

March 7

"Learn to sit back and observe, not everything needs a reaction. You call the shots and hold all the cards, so if something is making you jump to some crazy conclusion or seemingly forcing you to react a certain way, just hold back and keep it calm. You have the power."

Unknown

"I used to rise to every occasion, get drawn out in pointless arguments, heated debates and fights even, now if you tell me 1 +1 = 3 I say Yes, Ok, have a great day, Goodbye!"
#MyTruth

March 8

"Care about what other people think and you will always be their prisoner."

Lao Tzu.

"Fuck will I ever be so damaged and blind that when I reach out the only thing I feel is the unstable ladder of other people's opinions"
#MyTruth

March 9

"If you catch yourself BEGGING someone for.....human decency? a response? time together? clarity? respect? some compassion? some kindness? You need to take a step back and realize that you're begging someone for the bare minimum. That's ridiculous and beneath you. Fuck that".

Unknown

"You read right...Fuck that and Fuck them. You should never have to beg for what you deserve, and you certainly don't ever have to settle for less. Be prepared to eat alone if they can't bring anything to your table"
#MyTruth

March 10

"I'm really into girls without a sense of humor," said no one, ever"

Carol Porges

"Gimme a girl full of laughter and spirit over a girl with perfect tits and ass any day.....make me laugh, make my life"
#MyTruth

March 11

"Never lose sight of the fact that the ultimate goal is to be happy. Wealth, success, popularity, and accomplishment only make sense if they're serving that goal. If they're serving any other goal, the cost of achieving them will move you further away from the ultimate goal"

Steven Bartlett

"Having money and all the trappings of success is secondary to being happy. All the things that are free are all the things we really need. I'd rather be poor and happy then rich and miserable" #MyTruth

March 12

"Your calm mind is the ultimate weapon against your challenges. So relax."

Bryant McGill

"I never get good results outside of being composed and calm, if allow anyone or anything to mess with my meds im giving permission to help me fail. My calmness is my shield of which ive used and won many a battles"
#MyTruth

March 13

"Learn to slow down. Get lost intentionally. Observe how you judge both yourself and those around you."

Tim Ferriss

"I play the fool fi ketch wise"...shit sprinkled with glitter is still shit"

#MyTruth

March 14

"You wouldn't plant a seed and then dig it up every few minutes to see if it has grown. So why do you keep questioning yourself, your hard work and your decisions? Have patience, stop overthinking and keep watering your seeds."

Steven Bartlett

"Have faith in your dreams, their yours , don't be distracted or taken of course by scrupulous individuals, take your time, enjoy the dream and if you want those dreams to come true you must wake up"
#MyTruth

March 15

"The noble-minded are calm and steady. Little people are forever fussing and fretting"

Confucius

"I ignore the loudest person in the centre of the room and befriend the humble person in the corner"
#MyTruth

March 16

"Life is more enjoyable when you appreciate how temporary every moment is. Your brightest moments are temporary, so you must live in the moment when the sun is shining. Your darkest moments are temporary, so you must never give up when it is raining."

Steven Bartlett

"I live every day like it's my last, I laugh daily and thou I've had my fair share of dark times I knew they too would pass and still I rise"
#MyTruth

March 17

"Rest and be kind, you don't have to prove anything."

Jack Kerouac

"My name speaks for itself, let yours"
#MyTruth

March 18

"Life is a balance of holding on and letting go."

Rumi

"I'm still walking the tight rope with hope and faith, and insured by the cushions below me called family to soften my fall or if I choose to jump" #MyTruth

March 19

"Ego prevents you from learning from others. Envy prevents you from focusing on yourself. Anger prevents you from seeing clearly. Ignorance prevents you from making good decisions.
Fear prevents you from seizing opportunities.
Get rid of them all"

Unknown

"Anything that prevents my personal growth and progress will eventually damage me, so i rid myself of all things toxic and replenish my life with all that is blessed"

March 20

"Arguing is fine if you're arguing with the right person.
Toxic arguments are always YOU vs THEM.
Healthy arguments are YOU and THEM vs THE PROBLEM.
Don't waste energy arguing with anyone that cares more about protecting their fragile ego, than resolving the problem."

Unknown

"Problem, Cause, Solution ....that route or no route. I actually only hold debates with those of whom I see as equal...all others I simply apply teaching"
#MyTruth

March 21

"Sometimes... the only closure you need is the understanding that you deserve better..."

Trent Shelton

"Had to get rid of some of these shallow girls because I struggled to have a deep relationship with them"
#MyTruth

March 22

"We all make mistakes, have struggles, and even regret things in our past. But you are not your mistakes, you are not your struggles, and you are here now with the power to shape your day and your future."

Steve Maraboli

"Boy have I made some blunders in my past, but if I lived in my past I'd still be a dickhead, I live in the present and now im great"
#MyTruth

March 23

"Revel in your freedom. Live wholeheartedly, laugh loud, love much, spread joy, be truthful, and give yourself to everything."

Robert Holden

"People often ask what is it that makes me tick?, and I swear its nothing they usually imagine. It's simply the freedom to do what I want, when I want. Freedom starts with my spiritual over-standing and then everything else aligns itself. Once you've reached that stage then only then will you know you've landed safely"
#MyTruth

March 24

"Never go in search of love, go in search of life, and life will find you the love you seek."

atticus

"I used to chase girls like the last bus. When I found myself and focused on sourcing life itself, I bought the bus company and fell in love with buses"
#MyTruth

March 25

"Too often we underestimate the power of a touch, a smile, a kind word, an honest compliment or the smallest act of caring, all of which have the potential to turn a life around."

Leo Buscaglia

"Focus on the simple things in life, don't underestimate how big and important your small gestures can be, imagine the impact a small fly has on you in a big room, it's the same concept"
#MyTruth

March 26

"Here's to fresh Ginger Tea, sunshine, morning walks, blooming flowers, good books, my chats with the real ones and all the other simple but glorious pleasures of life"

Terence Wallen

"My Book, My Quote. Be grateful for your life's little pleasures, those are the things that really matter and will be missed significantly above all the big things we once thought was important"

March 27

"Don't let them water you down,
Don't ever get use to that bad taste,
Don't dilute your thing, Keep it
Fizzy"

Terence Wallen

"Never be afraid of being yourself and never let anything force you into being a version of you that you yourself don't recognise. You are who you are, no regrets, no excuses and no conforming. If they leave you still, you'll be calm but if they shake you up your entitled to explode"

March 28

"When you're different, sometimes you don't see the millions of people who accept you for what you are. All you notice is the person who does not."

Jodi Picoult

"Being different is a blessing, so I actually see and have time for those that love me and give a sweet "Fuck You" to those that don't"

March 29

"Time decides who you meet in life, your heart decides who you want in your life, and your behavior decide who stays in your life."

Unknown

"Appreciate those that you have before they become those you had"

March 30

"Life is funny. Things change, people change, but you will always be you, so stay true to yourself and never sacrifice who you are for anyone."

Zayn Malik

"When your real and only present the true you, the real ones will accept you"

March 31

"Some things cannot be taught; they must be experienced. You never learn the most valuable lessons in life until you go through your own journey."

Roy T. Bennett

"I've learnt more through experiences than I could ever of been taught, my life experiences has been the most, compelling, exciting and informative text book imaginable"

April

April 1

"The moment you become aware of the ego in you, it is strictly speaking no longer the ego, but just an old, conditioned mind-pattern. Ego implies unawareness. Awareness and ego cannot coexist."

Eckhart Tolle

"Once I got to know who I 'was', the 'was' in me resided. My greatness became my awareness"

April 2

"Success in life is founded upon attention to the small things rather than to the large things; to the every day things nearest to us rather than to the things that are remote and uncommon."

Booker T Washington

"People look at the pounds but don't recognise the pennies you had to go through to make the pounds, they see the street lights but totally ignore the stars, when in fact the street lights are minuscule compared to the stars"

April 3

"The challenge of leadership is to be strong but not rude; be kind, but not weak; be bold, but not a bully; be humble, but not timid; be proud, but not arrogant; have humor, but without folly."

Jim Rohn

"It's taken a lot of time, effort, challenges, work, commitment, sacrifices, patience and unconditional love to become the leader I am today, and with those very ingredients ill develop more leaders"

April 4

"As a person of power, your priority in life should be self-reliance:
Position of power where you depend on no one.
Most people are afraid to go on this path, to sink or swim on their own."

Unknown

"I thought that I didn't want anyone until I realised I needed someone. The world can be a lonely place, but it really does not have to be"

April 5

"Crying does not indicate that you are weak. Since birth, it has always been a sign that you are alive."

Charlotte Bronte

"It's ok to cry, its ok show vulnerability, don't hold in what your meant to let out"

April 6

"If your emotional abilities aren't in hand, if you don't have self-awareness, if you are not able to manage your distressing emotions, if you can't have empathy and have effective relationships, then no matter how smart you are, you are not going to get very far."

Daniel Goleman

"A real King must have all the attributes to hold up his Kingdom, a lack of what it takes will result in it being taken"

April 7

"Never allow someone to be your priority while allowing yourself to be their option."

MarkTwain

"I'm guilty of this over and over...until I'm over"

April 8

"It matters not who you love, where you love, why you love, when you love or how you love, it matters only that you love."

John Lennon

"I love who I want, when I want, how I want, you don't have to like it, but you may simply have to grow to love it"

April 9

"Respect is earned, Honesty is appreciated, Love is gained, and Loyalty is returned"

Unknown

"Do good and good will without doubt follow you, what you put out you will get in return 10-fold. Respect, Honesty, Love and Loyalty maketh the man"

April 10

"Quiet the mind, and the soul will speak."

Ma Jaya Sati Bhagavati

"I so want someone of whom I can communicate with purely via my soul, if you are out there and can hear me I'm speaking without words"

April 11

"Be tolerant of those who are lost on their path. Ignorance, conceit, anger, jealousy and greed stem from a lost soul. Pray that they will find guidance."

Elder Wisdom

"Haters will be haters, we simply have to accept that, but I truly believe that it's the hate of themselves that manifests itself and they know only to place it onto others, haters need a hug too"

April 12

"The ultimate measure of a man is not where he stands in moments of comfort and convenience, but where he stands at times of challenge and controversy"

Martin Luther King Jr.

"Your true colours will reveal itself in times of trouble or unease. On many occasions I have left my place of comfort and stepped into a place of conflict for the purpose of others, it's not easy but it's worth it...hence I'm measured"

April 13

"I AM GROUNDED. My spirit is grounded deep in the earth. I am calm, strong, centered and peaceful. I am able to let go of fear and trust that I am eternally safe. I am worthy of all things BEAUTIFUL."

Carly Marie

"I am, you are, if not...you Can be…. it's never too late. Change is good"

April 14

"The key to success is to keep growing in all areas of life - mental, emotional, spiritual, as well as physical."

Julius Erving

"Every day is a new day, don't repeat your days the same over and over calling that living. Embrace all aspects of growth, you must live, just being alive is not enough"

April 15

"The quality of your thinking determines the quality of your life."

A R Bernard

"We must take control of our thinking and ensure it's of the qualitative type so that it reflects on our life. By our thoughts we are lead what to say, what we then say can become the things we are willing to do, habits are now formed by what we say and do. So quality thinking will result in a quality life"

April 16

"God does not give you the people you want, he gives you the people you need. To help you, to hurt you, to leave you, to love you and to make you the person you were meant to be."

Unknown

"Everybody who ever entered my life served a purpose, be it good or bad they served me... chronicles of a King"

April 17

"Your beliefs become your thoughts.
Your thoughts become your words.
Your words become your actions.
Your actions become your habits.
Your habits become your values.
Your values become your destiny.
The future depends on what you do today."

Mahatma Gandhi

"I had to stand for something in order to stand out. No way was I to be gifted with life from my mother's womb and not be of a great contribution to life itself. I stand today tall with my values of yesterday so i could prepare for tomorrow"

April 18

"The biggest mistake I made in the past was that I believed love was about finding the right person. In reality, love is about becoming the right person. Don't look for the person you want to spend your life with. Become the person you want to spend your life with."

Neil Strauss

"I had to date a fare few women in search for Mrs Right, only to realise that I wasn't right myself. So I may have found and lost her because I was too busy trying to perfect her instead of perfecting myself. Lucky is she now who finds me, now that I've found myself" (women of no substance need not apply).

April 19

"I cried because I had no shoes until I met a man who had no feet."

Helen Keller

"I have learnt to appreciate and show continuous gratitude for what I have, knowing full well that even my least can be of plenty to the next man. Take nothing for granted as that one day can also be taken"

April 20

"100 years ago everyone owned a horse and only the rich had cars. Today everyone has a car and only the rich own horses."

Unknown

"How shit has changed and will flip like a coin again. The world will not be the same and we must be prepared for it. With a little saving or good credit we can all now afford horses, it's no longer just for the rich, you simply have to want one and willing to do what it takes to get one, don't limit your reach...thou parking may prove a problem"

April 21

"Just because you are starting in life from modest background does not mean you need to remain your whole life as such. As someone aiming for power, one of your long-term goals should be financial independence. By doing well for yourself you'll be able to do well for other people"

Poweropedia

"I refuse to be a product of my environment, instead I choose to make my environment a product of me. My legacy will remain in the minds & hearts of many well after I have departed"

April 22

"The greatest battles of life are fought out daily in the silent chambers of the soul..."

David O. McKay

"It's the battles and the pains no one can see or feel but you, all those inner battles we have to fight, then still have to deal with the external dramas of life. Work on your inner battles first, they will dictate how you handle the outer ones"

April 23

"If you win battles there (within), everything becomes easier. Self-mastery is the highest form of power that human beings can reach."

Unknown

"The self-power is the self we know, only when we have mastered ourselves can we then attempt to prove as masters of other things. I knew I was masterful once I became my own master and took instructions and directions from myself"

April 24

"I am not a product of my circumstances. I am a product of my decisions."

Stephen Covey

"The situations I found myself in of which i was to blame or accept fault was solely down to my poor decision making, circumstances will always present themselves the way I choose to deal with those circumstances is solely down to me....I no longer blame my circumstances"

April 25

"When we are no longer able to change a situation, we are challenged to change ourselves."

Victor Frankl

I've found myself in many situations including relationships that changing the state of play seemed way beyond me, so instead of changing the other person I instead changed myself....and took the better version of me and left"

April 26

"Trust takes years to build, seconds to break, and forever to repair. A single lie discovered is enough to create doubt in every truth expressed."

Unknown

"Once bitten twice shy my mum always said, she also told me that 'Every liar is a thief and every thief is a liar'...with that said my trust issues will remain whilst you still remain"

April 27

"Freedom is not worth having if it does not include the freedom to make mistakes."

Mahatma Gandhi

"It's said you learn best from your mistakes; we only fall over so we can learn to get back up, the freedom to make mistakes is the freedom to learn"

April 28

"Our lives begin to end the day we become silent about things that matter."

Martin Luther King, Jr.

"We must always speak our truth, all the greats before us spoke up for what they believed, ill follow suit and become great also"

April 29

"If you can't fly then run, if you can't run then walk, if you can't walk then crawl, but whatever you do you have to keep moving forward."

Martin Luther King Jr.

"Never give up on your dreams, regardless how long it seems to be taking, be a snail if you must just don't be a statue"

April 30

"The right person will make you a priority. If you find yourself feeling like you're not good enough, it is because they're not good enough."

Steve Maraboli

"I'm at my best when I'm with you, your contribution to my life and existence has contributed to who I am today. If at any point you feel like I'm not good enough for you it's because you have failed loving yourself and in return can't love me either"

May

May 1

"The most beautiful people I've known are those who have known trials, have known struggles, have known loss, and have found their way out of the depths."

Elisabeth Kübler-Ross

"I know myself, I know my Mother, I know my daughter, all of whom signify beauty in every possible way through the ugly struggle"

May 2

"Be around the light bringers, the
magic makers, the world shifters, the
game shakers.
They challenge you, break you open,
uplift and expand you.
They don't let you play small with
your life.
These heartbeats are your people.
These people are your tribe"

Danielle Doby

"My Tribe, My Village, My People, My World... without them I am nothing, no man is an island and if I was i'd have all these very same people on it with me. Appreciate and show gratitude always to your real ones because they are so rare"

May 3

"Find people who can handle your darkest truths, who don't change the subject when you share your pain, or try to make you feel bad for feeling bad. Find people who understand we all struggle, some of us more than others, and that there's no weakness in admitting it. In fact, few things take as much strength.
Find people who want to be real, however that looks and feels, and who want you to be real, too.
Find people who get that life is hard, and who get that life is also beautiful, and who aren't afraid to honor both those realities. Find people who help you feel more at home in your heart, mind and body, and who take joy in your joy. Find people who love you, for real, and who accept you, for real. Just as you are. They're out there, these people. Your tribe is waiting for you. Don't stop searching until you find them"

Scott Stabile

"I've found them, you can find them, and they will also help you to find yourself.... this is the find we've all been searching for"

May 4

"Some people arrive and make such a beautiful impact on your life, you can barely remember what life was like without them".

Unknown

"I often think what my life would have been like and how different it would of been had it not been for an handful of people, I'm so grateful for their existence in my existence"

May 5

"Remember, you don't need a certain number of friends. just a number of friends you can be certain of".

Unknown

"Less means more and Quality over quantity always. Keep your circle tight, you actually don't need the numbers, you don't need to be surrounded by 'Yes people', believe me they will be around you when the going is good, but when the good has gone so will they be"

May 6

"A friend is someone who listens to your bullshit, tells you that it is bullshit and listens some more"

Unknown

"Lolol, yeah I have those friends I have to listen to…Raj, Omar, Sacha, Saf, Avtar, Althea, Matty, Christine, Maxine, David..…the list goes on lol… so that's my friends who's BS im obligated to listen to…..Start making your list below now"

May 7

"I avoid shit because my temper can go from 0 to life in prison in 2 seconds"

Unknown

"Sometimes it's better to just walk away....and pay a hitman"

May 8

"Anyone who is in love is making love the whole time, even when they're not. When two bodies meet, it is just the cup overflowing. They can stay together for hours, even days. They begin the dance one day and finish it the next, or--such is the pleasure they experience--they may never finish it"

Paulo Coelho

"When that connection is made you ask yourself wtf was you doing in some previous relationships, some relationships make you feel things you never thought you would and things you never thought you could. Love to love!"

May 9

"I believe that sex is one of the most beautiful, natural, wholesome things that money can buy lol"

Steve Martin

"I have never bought sex in my life, but it has cost me dearly"

May 10

"I've personally never paid for sex, but i would just so I can experience swiping my credit card between her thighs and waiting to see where the receipts going to come from."

Terence Wallen

"Since writing that quote, we've moved onto to contactless payment, now we can literally "Tap that Ass & go"

May 11

"Anyone who thinks sitting in church can make you a Christian must also think that sitting in a garage can make you a car."

Garrison Keillor

"No matter where you are, be yourself, pick the sense out the nonsense and don't be fooled by people's surroundings. Not everyone in court is guilty and not everyone found not guilty is innocent. Places rarely change that's why we have to"

May 12

"Go to heaven for the climate and hell for the company"

Benjamin Franklin Wade

"See you there....yes you, see you there, lol. Where? I hear you ask, we'll talk when we get there i responded" (acting like you know where your going from here)."

May 13

"Shut back di pot, wash out you plate, if you tek me plate bring it back, dat bowl older dan you, weh u woman deh weh fi cook fi you? Come come time fi unnuh gwome"

Gloria Wallen

"Those words of our parents will resonate with us forever and will be the soundtracks of our lives. To think on initially hearing them spouted at me from my mother for years, id roll my eyes and think omg… now I hear myself saying them to my own kids, but I can't see their eyes because they too busy in their phones.. my mum thou"

May 14

“She never gets tired of saying it and ill never escape it”

Terence Wallen

“Woman who repeat themselves year in year out... or is it me not changing year in year out?”

May 15

"Yes Dad" ..- My Children ("Your children must at all times show you the ultimate respect, being a parent is the ultimate sacrifice and you can't repay me with so ill settle for manners"

Terence Wallen

"No sentence, no eye contact, no nothing would continue unless we 1st got pass those 2 little words that always lived together in my presence. No 'Yes Dad' when I call your name, nothing more from me"

May 16

"Like music to my ears, I can never get tired of hearing it"

#MyTruth

"It's like the on switch in my head, shut off everything until I hear the right words. You may have the ability to speak to me but only the selected can speak into me"

May 17

"A successful man is one who can lay a firm foundation with the bricks others have thrown at him."

David Brinkley

"Every attempt to stop me has failed, every word spoke against me has become wind and every brick thrown at me or in my direction has been collected and used to build what is now my empire"

May 18

"There are two types of people who will tell you that you cannot make a difference in this world: those who are afraid to try and those who are afraid you will succeed."

Ray Goforth

"Fuck anyone who tells you that you can't, only you can stop yourself. The time they take to tell you that you can't they could have tried themselves. They fear your greatness.... before it happens and what it will look like once it does"

May 19

"By recording your dreams and goals on paper, you set in motion the process of becoming the person you most want to be. Put your future in good hands — your own."

Mark Victor Hansen

"Trust and believe in yourself, be your own cheerleader, be your own teacher, have that conversation with yourself and ask yourself who am i not to be bloody great"

May 20

"Do what you have to do until you can do what you want to do."

Oprah Winfrey

"This is where I'm at, that place called freedom, the place that when you reach makes it all feel worth it, i did things other people wouldn't now I'm doing things other people can't"

May 21

"Women cannot complain about men anymore until they start getting better taste in them."

Bill Maher

"Exactly...stop calling him shit when it was you who picked him up, which in that case makes you a poop bag!! Nothing will change until you do, if you go for the same kind of guys expect the same kind of results"

May 22

"Stop telling me shit about the man you chose after me, you knew he was no good in the beginning, you chased the hype now he's not your type.... quit complaining, leave or shut the fuck up and stay unhappy"

#MyTruth

"I say poetically to my ex when she is full of regret and wants me back, Please!!! The grass was not greener on the other side, actually there was no grass it was just weeds"

May 23

"Nothing in the world can take the place of Persistence. Talent will not; nothing is more common than unsuccessful men with talent. Genius will not; unrewarded genius is almost a proverb. Education will not; the world is full of educated derelicts. Persistence and determination alone are omnipotent. The slogan 'Press On' has solved and always will solve the problems of the human race."

Calvin Coolidge

"Amen to that, make sure giving up is never an option, even when you have failed it means you're trying. Don't give up"

May 24

"Pain is temporary. It may last a minute, or an hour, or a day, or a year, but eventually it will subside and something else will take its place. If I quit, however, it lasts forever."

Lance Armstrong

"The scars mean you have healed, let that be a reminder that you've survived. They may have won the battle, but they have not won the war. Quitters will never win, and a winner will never quit"

May 25

"Death is not the opposite of life, but a part of it"

Haruki Murakam

"Amen...I've learnt that recently, took some time to understand it but I got there"

May 26

"We all die. The goal isn't to live forever, the goal is to create something that will"

Chuck Palahniuk

"So I'm working on my legacy, I've worked tirelessly to connect with my true purpose to ensure my legacy is enjoyed and celebrated forever, what I leave behind, my life's work will benefit future generations and that will be my passing gift to the world"

May 27

"If your life improves the lives of even 5 people, then your life is successful, but if you live even a 100 years, earning millions of pounds, without willingly improving the life of even one person, then your entire life is a waste."

Abhijit Naskar

"My purpose of life is to live a life of purpose, I lead not for fame or gratification but so I can build more leaders not a mass a great following. If we cannot impact other lives positively then what is our lives?"

May 28

"There's no shortage of remarkable ideas, what's missing is the will to execute them."

Seth Godin

"Don't just dream, wake up, Don't just say, do and don't just think it, take risks and do it, you will never know unless you try, if you don't try then it was merely a dream that may as well as been a nightmare for all you did with it"

May 29

"Try not to become a person of success, but rather try to become a person of value."

Albert Einstein

"When you are only a success your value is material, and you know the price of everything and the real value of nothing. Be a person of value and you can never lose your worth"

May 30

"I've learned that people will forget what you said, people will forget what you did, but people will never forget how you made them feel."

Maya Angelou

"I've already forgotten some of the things my mum, my children, my partners and my real friends have said over the years, but I can't ever forget how they made me feel. Words spoken will come and go; the things we did can also be forgotten and those memories over time can fade away, however, the everlasting emotion" created in a situation that penetrates the core of our feelings tends to stay with us forever"

May 31

"Someone is sitting in the shade today because someone planted a tree a long time ago."

Warren Buffett

"I never forget those that came before me, allowed me to stand tall on their shoulders, laid the foundations for me to build on, planted those very trees so I could sit in the shade comfortably, dimmed their own lights so mine could shine and cleared the path so I could see where I was going....that someone is my brother Sted" R.I.E.P (1960 - 2017)"

June

June 1

"It does not matter how slowly you go, so long as you do not stop."

Confucius

"We all have our destinations and different arrival times; thou time waits on no one our journeys within that time will vary. Follow not the next persons schedule, stick to your speed it's your journey and you will arrive"

June 2

"You only live once, but if you do it right, once is enough."

Mae West

"Actually I think you can live loads and you only die once.... do not limit your living capacity.... being alive is One, Living is much more"

June 3

"The longer I live, the more beautiful life becomes."

Frank Lloyd Wright

"I am the architect of my life and what I build is incomparably beautiful"

June 4

"You can't please everyone, and you can't make everyone like you."

Katie Couric

"I care zero if you like me, the real ones love me, I have no intention to attempt to please everyone and of that I'm extremely pleased"

June 5

"I believe every human has a finite number of heartbeats. I don't intend to waste any of mine."

Neil Armstrong

"Live every day like it's your last, because it actually could be"

June 6

"Don't limit yourself. Many people limit themselves to what they think they can do. You can go as far as your mind lets you. What you believe, remember, you can achieve."

Mary Kay Ash

"Speak it into existence , throw it out into the universe, stretch your mind, write them down, tick them off as you go along, don't hold back, anything you put your mind to you can achieve, as long as you believe"

June 7

"If your actions inspire others to dream more, learn more, do more and become more, you are a leader."

John Quincy Adams

"As a leader, I don't need more followers, i need more leaders, to help me build more leaders who in turn will build more leaders....that's what real leadership creates"

June 8

"I am hoping that in this year of the family we will go into our families and reconcile differences"

Louis Farrakhan

"Nothing happens before its time; we don't have to see eye to eye but we will always see heart to heart. Thou I must add not all family is good and the differences can remain as they are, and they can keep a respectable distance"

June 9

"The more you praise and celebrate your life, the more there is in life to celebrate."

Oprah Winfrey

"Accept & celebrate your greatness and that within itself will make you feel great"

June 10

"Being confident is the key to life. Don't be afraid to be you! I'm super different from a lot of men, my confidence, my style, my personality, positive outlook on all things and my choice to live my life how i choose.... and I'm OK with it. Just be yourself cos they cant be you."

Unknown

"Believe in yourself, nothing is impossible, you can achieve anything you put your mind too. Remember you lack nothing and you are everything"
#MyTruth

June 11

"Either write something worth reading or do something worth writing."

Benjamin Franklin

"Well your reading this and I wrote it.... I rest my case, the proof is in your hand"
#MyTruth

June 12

"Find out who you are and be that person. That's what your soul was put on this Earth to be. Find that truth, live that truth and everything else will come."

Ellen DeGeneres

"I realised who I was when being me was the only thing I was absolutely good at. When you call on your truths everything comes running" #MyTruth

June 13

"The best way to not feel hopeless is to get up and do something. Don't wait for good things to happen to you. If you go out and make some good things happen, you will fill the world with hope, you will fill yourself with hope."

Barack Obama

"Don't procrastinate, time waits on no one, everything you've ever wanted is on the other side of fear, embrace faith and hope, live in the present, your greatness already exists, let it shine so other too will want to be great"
#MyTruth

June 14

"If something is important enough, even if the odds are against you, you should still do it."

Elon Musk

"Follow your heart, do what's right even if no one else is doing it. You cannot live someone else's life so you may as well live yours how you wish" #MyTruth

June 15

"Be fearless. Have the courage to take risks. Go where there are no guarantees. Get out of your comfort zone even if it means being uncomfortable. The road less travelled is sometimes fraught with barricades, bumps, and uncharted terrain. But it is on that road where your character is truly tested. Have the courage to accept that you'rc not perfect, nothing is and no one is — and that's OK."

Katie Couric

'I couldn't of said it better, so read it as if you had said it and feel better"

June 16

"Listen to silence. It has so much to say."

Rumi

"Silence speaks volumes and saying nothing can be so loud. I speak with the voice in my head daily and what a pleasant conversation we have"

June 17

"Saying nothing sometimes says the most."

Emily Dickinson

"..............................."!!!!
#MyTruth

June 18

"When you have nothing to say, say nothing."

Charles Caleb Colton

"Simply STFU, daaam nobody wants to hear your Bullshit, even the deaf don't wanna hear it"

June 19

“Life, if well lived, is long enough”

Seneca

“I don’t believe in the afterlife, so I’m doing all my good whilst living here”

June 20

"Melanin is an incomparable beauty. From the lightest to the darkest skin tone, black women are exquisite beauty in every shade. Yes, black females have that special something that just can't be ignored. We are melanin queens, beautifully created! respect the complexion."

SL

"I so love my Queens, my Mother, my Sisters, my Kids mums, all my relatives, my past girlfriends and present one.....they ooze beauty, they ooze blackness, they ooze everything that stands for beautiful. I want nothing more but to love them cos I love myself and i am them"

June 21

"I'm convinced that we black women possess a special indestructible strength that allows us to not only get down, but to get up, get through, and to get over."

Janet Jackson

"The Diary of every strong black woman, you won't go unrecognised, we feel you, we hear you, we see you, we love you, we need you"

June 22

"A small body of determined spirits fired by an unquenchable faith in their mission can alter the course of history"

Mahatma Gandhi

"Quality over quantity all day every day. I had a small team with minimal resources that made more of a global difference because we were rich with faith and desire for change more so than the big corporations who with all their resources proved inadequate"

June 23

"I want history to remember me... not as the black man to have set up a charity specifically supporting African Caribbean's living with HIV/AIDS, or the black man who sponsored a number of struggling schools in Jamaica or the black man who set up a project mobilising medical care to the people in rural Malawi Africa or the black man who mentored countless young men & women in the UK who became beacons of light... but as a black man who lived in the 20th century and who dared to be himself. I want to be remembered as a catalyst for change."

Terence Wallen

"When I exit this earth, as long as I'm remembered for being me, I wont haunt you"

June 24

"Don't be so hard on yourself. Be perfectly okay with being who YOU are. Fully embrace yourself, flaws and all. Love yourself right where you are. Strive to do better, but don't beat yourself up for every shortcoming that you may have. Be brave in your journey! Hold your head up high, and keep moving forward"

Stephanie Lahart

"Love yourself, warts, flaws and all, embrace your imperfect imperfections. Once we know better, we can do better. We are all born of sin and how boring life would have been if we never used up some of them"

June 25

"Dear Black Queens - Never underestimate the beauty of just being YOU. Being your authentic self is powerful, sexy, and courageous!"

Stephanie Lahart

"Dear Black Kings - Never underestimate the strength of just being YOU. Being your naturally great self is empowering, beautiful and awesome"

June 26

"Ok...so if your not Black then amend it to suit yourself, if your male then share it with the queen you know....if you are a black queen then just know the quote is all yours and I unapologetically adore you x"

Terence Wallen

"Yeah I said it without apology, I have my personal preferences, be not afraid to live & speak your truth"

June 27

"We don't stop playing because we grow old. We grow old because we stop playing."

George Bernard Shaw

"Sometimes I act childish and immature because that's how I feel, if you don't like it then don't let it bother you because I have no intention of changing anytime soon and the way I feel in body & mind it seems I'll be here for some time acting the same way"

June 28

"There is a fountain of youth: it is your mind, your talents, the creativity you bring to your life and the lives of people you love. When you learn to tap this source, you will truly have defeated age."

Sophia Loren

"People always say 'I look good for my age'.... well thank you, I feel great for my age, I stopped counting the years and ensured I made all the years count"
#MyTruth

June 29

"I believe the second half of one's life is meant to be better than the first half. The first half is finding out how you do it. And the second half is enjoying it."

Frances Lear

'First I heard the music then I started to dance. Definitely living the best half of my life once i realised that latter half had less restrictions and more experiences. As I age gracefully I met freedom who has now become my best friend"

June 30

"I love living. I love that I'm alive to love my age. There are many people who went to bed just as I did yesterday evening and didn't wake this morning. I love and feel very blessed that I did."

Maya Angelou

"Forever grateful and thankful for life itself. Even on my most shit days i show gratitude. I am in love with life itself and all that I›ve been blessed with. We must not take something as normal as breathing for granted, someone somewhere just took their last breath"

July

July 1

"Learn the difference between connection and attachment. Connection gives you power, Attachment sucks the life out of you"

Unknown

"When my spirit is aligned with yours our connection is beautiful and the natural energy flows. When I feel I'm attached to you I feel stuck, restricted and drained when trying to free myself"

July 2

"The less you associate with some people, the more your life will improve. Any time you tolerate mediocrity in others, it increases your mediocrity. An important attribute in successful people is their impatience with negative thinking and negative acting people. As you grow, your associates will change. Some of your friends will not want you to go on. They will want you to stay where they are. Friends that don't help you climb will want you to crawl. Your friends will stretch your vision or choke your dream. Those that don't increase you will eventually decrease you"

Colin Powell

"My life got better the moment I removed myself from all things and persons that were toxic. Remaining in the same negative circle will only produce negative outcomes. Some of your so-called friends don't actually like you, they like the benefit to them that you serve. Don't entertain these parasites, having them in your life is the equivalent to drinking poison slowly, regardless it's going to destroy you"

July 3

"You either say how you feel & fuck it up or say nothing & let it fuck you up instead"

Unknown

"You say it & fuck it up I say, what use are you when you've been fucked up. In a gun battle it's not who draws 1st, its who shoots on target 1st, so do what you got to do to ensure the win"

July 4

"Accept what you can't change and change what you can't accept"

Unknown

"It has to start from within, when you change yourself and your thinking you then change how you see things. Never worry about the things you can't control and manage well the things you can"

July 5

"Close some doors today. Not because of pride, incapacity or arrogance, but simply because they lead you nowhere."

Paulo Coelho

"Somethings simply have to come to an end ...goodbye, Au revoir , Adios....Fuck off"

July 6

"Sometimes you need to let go of your niceness and show your brutal side, the side difficult to deal with. If you're always compliant you will encourage people to push and push and treat you worse than you deserve. Have boundaries that no one can cross"

Unknown

"I'm guilty of letting people take my kindness for weakness, I'm a sucker for saying Yes and helping people I should actually say No too. However, I believe my blessing await me and the boundaries I'm yet to set also opens me up for further blessings"

July 7

"The secret of change is to focus all of your energy, not on fighting the old, but on building the new."

Socrates

"Change is for the future because that's the way you're going, fixing the past is like walking backwards and no one does that for long and gets anywhere"

July 8

"The purpose of life is not solely to be happy. It is also to be useful, to be honorable, to be compassionate, to have it make some difference that you have lived and lived well. "

Ralph Waldo Emerson

"The purpose of life is to live that life of purpose. The pleasures of life are not only in living for ourselves but for the living we do for others. I made a difference by being different. I will have no regrets when the almighty calls me"

July 9

"A soulmate isn't someone who completes you. A soulmate is someone who inspires you to complete yourself; who loves you with so much conviction and so much heart, that never doubt just how capable you are of becoming exactly who you have always wanted to be."

Bianca Sparacino

"I got my soulmates.... yes plural...soulmates!!! .... they push me to greatness and when i reach there I will reach back and pull them all up with me. My soulmates are better than yours"

July 10

"The best day of your life is when you decide your life is your own. No apologies or excuses. No one to lean on, rely on, or blame. The gift is yours–it is an amazing journey–and you alone are responsible for the quality of it. It is the day your life really begins."

Bob Moawad

"You must take responsibility for you, accept all those flaws so they can't be used against you, embrace and celebrate your greatness and accept its all you also. Decide from this day onwards that it's a new day, focus solely on the things you now want, not on the things you never got"

July 11

"The world makes way for the man who knows where he is going."

Ralph Waldo Emerson

"Knowing where you are going is so much easier when you know from where you came. How shit it would be to be on a journey to nowhere knowing that you will never reach. Have your destination in mind if even not in sight"

July 12

"I've found that nothing in life is worthwhile unless you take risks. Fall forward. Every failed experiment is one step closer to success. Never be discouraged. Never look back. Give everything you've got. And when you fall throughout life, fall forward."

Denzel Washington

"Take calculated risks because even if it does not work then at least you can say you tried, and you've learnt. To not take risks is not to have lived"

July 13

"Be present. I would encourage you with all my heart just to be present. Be present and open to the moment that is unfolding before you. Because, ultimately, your life is made up of moments. So don't miss them by being lost in the past or anticipating the future."

Jessica Lange

"It's literally now or never, I've never appreciated the 'Now' so much as I do at this present time. Losing someone who had plans and numerous aspirations but never lived long enough to have fulfilled them as taught me to live in the present, it's not enough to just dream, one has to wake up in order for dreams to come true. Tomorrow may never come, but if it does do something worthwhile with it as it literally can be your last"

July 14

"Intelligence without ambition is a bird without wings."

Salvador Dali

"What is the use of being intelligent but with no desire to use put that intelligence to good use? Without ambition it makes no difference how clever or educated you are, that's why still have educated fools with wasted potential because the lack in ambition. Ambition does not mean you will become a millionaire or CEO of a corporation it just means you are willing to make that move to better yourself and even those around you. Sometimes those of us that are intelligent just need a little nudge or support in the direction of ambition from others to realise our true potential"

July 15

"Distance yourself from negative people who try to lower your motivation and decrease your ambition. Create space for positive people to come into your life.
Surround yourself with positive people who believe in your dreams, encourage your ideas, support your ambitions, and bring out the best in you".

Roy T Bennett

"Nothing or no one toxic needs to be in your life...period. There is no room for them, nore no time for them. They mean you no good, they will smile at you but deep down they wish for your downfall. Learn to spot them from early, follow your inner spirit and listen to inner voice, trust your intuition, and gut feelings, its usually right. Waste not a minute of your life with those that don't bring out the best in you, spend that time instead with those that see the greatness in you, even if your yet to see it in yourself. Remember if you fill your life with negative people you leave no room for the positive ones to enter"

July 16

"What do you mean I have to wait for someone's approval? *I'm* someone. *I* approve. So I give myself permission to move forward with my full support!"

Richelle E Goodrich

"I'm my own boss, once a accept me then that's all the acceptance needed. I'll interview myself and give myself the job telling myself I'm the best person I've seen all day"

July 17

"The struggles we endure today will be the 'good old days' we laugh about tomorrow."

Aaron Lauritsen

"We will face hardships and struggles on this journey called life, but this will be temporary and too will pass. We will look back and say 'Wow, I've come a long way, and because of the lessons learnt that's made me into a better person it was certainly a road worth travelling'. Sometimes we have to go through the losses to appreciate the wins"

July 18

"I'm tough, I'm ambitious, and I know exactly what I want. If that makes me a too much, then okay!"

Terence Wallen

"Yeah...I'm ok with being me and just as ok with you not liking me. Better to be too much than not enough. Not everyone is going to be happy with your greatness or success...but who cares? I do not."
#MyTruth

July 19

"Whether it is the best of times or the worst of times, it is the only time we've got."

Art Buchwald

"They say, 'Time is the master', but what they should say is that 'We must be the master of our time'. Make use of time, because once it's gone its gone and there is no getting it back"
#MyTruth

July 20

"Sometimes it takes getting pushed to the edge before you can find your voice to speak out; it takes hitting the rock bottom to realize you're done descending, and it is time to rise; it takes being made to feel like you're nothing to help you see that you are complete."

Mandy Hale

"Your journey is yours, take the highs with the lows, just give thanks and be grateful that you are here to have a journey"

July 21

"Until you let go of all the toxic people or situations in your life you will never be able to grow into your fullest potential. Let them go so you can grow."

DLQ

"My mother used to say ‹Show me your company and I'll tell you who you are' , the same goes with negative and toxic situations, remove them or it's so easy to become like them. The weight of negativity will restrict your movements"

July 22

"'Restore connection' is not just for devices, it is for people too. If we cannot disconnect, we cannot lead."

Arianna Huffington

"You have to be close enough to motivate but far enough ahead to lead"

July 23

"The way to achieve your own success is to be willing to help somebody else get it first."

Iyanla Vanzant

"The more you put out will be the more you get back, helping others will in turn help you to help yourself. My success is measured by the success gained by others of whom I›ve had an influence"

July 24

"We must believe that we are gifted for something, and that this thing, at whatever cost, must be attained."

Marie Curie

"Believe you are here for a purpose and live that purpose. Don't ever give up on your dreams, work through the struggles, fight the good fight, your rewards await you"

July 25

"The difference between greed and ambition is a greedy person desires things he isn't prepared to work for."

Habeeb Akande

"I come across greedy people all the time, they want what they wasn›t willing to graft for, they see what you have but don›t see the work, the struggles, the sacrifices you›ve had to make to achieve what you have. Greedy people will never succeed"

July 26

"Realising your ambitions, controlling your fate, and achieving unrivaled greatness is derived from knowing what to change, how to change, and, most importantly, why to change"

Dean Gualco

"Change is good. Without change you will simply remain"

July 27

"If everybody likes you, you have a serious problem. Not all will love you. There will always be some who hate you for no reason or without even knowing you. That's Life. Smile and move on..."

Frank M Gashumba

"I care zero who does not like me, I care only for those that love me. Its ok to be disliked once you realise that most people that dislike you actually don't like themselves"

July 28

"When you hurt us, take it as loan… because we will bring it back with interest. And you good people, everybody isn't going like or love you. Most people don't even love themselves. Nothing in the world is more dangerous than sincere HATE and conscientious ENVY."

Frank M Gashumba

"Be careful of wolves in sheep clothing, they will smile with you just moments before they destroy you. When your heart is clean and the wicked fight against you, fear not.... the Almighty will deal with them, so you don't have to"

July 29

"When you build in silence, Haters & Loosers don't know what to attack. Some people will never support you because they are afraid of what you might become and some people will only check on you just to see if you have failed."

Frank M Gashumba

"The more you show the more they can see, and not everyone is looking to congratulate you. Look out for those who do not clap when you are worthy of applause. Some people will go through every effort to keep you down and will use all their efforts to ensure you stay there......be aware of these people"

July 30

"I only debate my equals. All others, i teach..."

John Henrik Clarke

"I value time more than anything, I value those with the same heart, morals and characteristics as myself. So with all similar values I will engage with the likeminded and I'm aware I will not have the same level if dialogue with those lacking, in which case I have to use the valuable time to teach them of the specific values"

July 31

"Happiness is the best revenge, because nothing drives your enemies more insane than seeing you smiling and living a good life." And Some people will never support you because they are afraid of what you might become."

Unknown

"My daily happiness has filled many a mental institution filled with those who can't deal with my success and love of life"

August

August 1

"It is fine if you don't like me not everyone has Good Taste"
#MyTruth

Terence Wallen

"I'm so daam comfortable in my own skin, I'm thinking of putting out a clothing range that only fits me lolol, and I've got such good taste I ask myself out"

August 2

"Never Forget Those Who Helped You On Your Way Up and "To care for those who once cared for us is one of the highest honors"

Inspired by Tia Walker

"Being able to repay those who have built me or who›s shoulders I stood on to now be able to stand tall is my ultimate aim, I'm so grateful and I let my team know this at every opportunity"

August 3

"I want to help you, but you have to be a willing participant. If you're not, then I am no longer helping you up; it is you who is pulling me down."

Steve Maraboli

"I can only do so much for any individual and I'm willing to help you come up, but I can't do all the pulling you up out the darkness if your not will to be part of the climbing out, I will eventually get weak pulling you out and may just fall in the darkness with you...and then what?"

August 4

"Here's a reminder for you:
i. Don't chase anyone.
ii. Don't beg someone to stay.
iii. Know your worth.
iv. Save space for people who matter.
v. Accept what cannot be changed.
vi. Leave what isn't for you.
vii. Love yourself."

Unknown Author

"To ensure you get the balance right and not allow negativity within your space I›d recommend you have daily positive affirmations, think, say, read, write, watch, speak of, say you're the best version of yourself, I am loved and I love others, I am beautiful, I am worthy, I am blessed" ..... positive thinking equals positive outcomes. Try it, trust me, you will see the difference in every day, the negativity then has no space to enter your thinking"

August 5

"Be the change that you wish to see in the world"

Mahatma Gandhi

"Lead by example, don't just speak of the things you want changed, become the change that you crave"

August 6

"Life is a series of natural and spontaneous changes. Don't resist them; that only creates sorrow. Let reality be reality. Let things flow naturally forward in whatever way they like"

Lao Tzu

"I used to focus so much on the future but now I just live for now as tomorrow isn't promised to no one. I accept everything that comes my way as part of my journey. I am present and it is where I reside"

August 7

"A wise man changes his mind, a fool never will"

Unknown

"Leave your mind open, be ready to learn as life never stops teaching, be not like the fool who thinks he knows it all"

August 8

"Please think about your legacy, because you're writing it every day"

Gary Vaynerchuck

"Every day you are given the gift of life you are given the chance to do something good. Be sure to do all good things today so you will be remembered of fondly tomorrow"

August 9

"Have you ever heard the sun come out in the morning? Did you hear the moon come out last night? We have been taught that power is loud, forceful, aggressive, and somewhat intimidating. It is not. In silence the Creator works."

Iyanla Vanzant

"Sometimes your silence says the most and it is that what speaks volumes. The Almighty is working tirelessly in your favour even in times you don't realise. Stay humble and you will hear everything that's meant for your soul to hear"

August 10

"In the eyes of man, a single bad deed can wipe out all the good you've done. But to the Almighty, a single good deed can wipe out all the bad you've done. He's the Most Forgiving, Most Merciful! Focus on pleasing Him for you can never please others, no matter how hard you try!"

Mufti Menk

"No matter how much good you do some people will only remember the one bad you did. It's like giving someone all the time and the one time you say no they say your mean. You can't always please people so its best you focus on pleasing yourself. In addition to that have faith in your creator not in man"
#MyTruth

August 11

"Keep people in your life that truly love you, motivate you, encourage you, inspire you, enhance you and make you happy"

Unknown

"Choose your circle wisely, better to can count your friends and have friends you can count on, than can't count them nor count on them" #MyTruth

August 12

"It is impossible to be negative when you're grateful.
It is impossible to criticize and blame when you're grateful.
It is impossible to feel sad or have any negative feeling when you're grateful. Gratitude unlocks a lot of happiness."

Unknown

"Once you're are grateful your open all doors to happiness. Being grateful for everything little thing means you appreciate everything you have and worry not of the things you don't have" #MyTruth

August 13

"Unless a man undertakes more than he possibly can do, he will never do all he can do."

Henry Drummond

"No one ever achieves by remaining in their comfort zone. Push yourself outside of your limits to attain more than you thought you would or could"
#MyTruth

August 14

"It always seems impossible until it is done"

Nelson Mandela

"We simply have to be willing to take risks, follow your dreams, go for it, make the once impossible, possible"
#MyTruth

August 15

"If we as a people realized the greatness from which we came we would be less likely to disrespect ourselves. Intelligence rules the world, ignorance carries the burden"

Marcus Garvey

"Rise up and recognise your greatness. We are here for a purpose, live that purpose. Do not allow anyone to ever and I repeat 'Ever' tell you that you can't achieve greatness"
#MyTruth

August 16

"Positivity can help you:
Heal yourself.
Find yourself.
Know yourself.
Correct yourself.
Love yourself.
Be yourself.
Respect yourself."

Unknown

"You›ll be surprised how just having a consistent positive attitude can change every aspect of your life without effort. Positive thinking leads to positive outcomes"

August 17

"Loving yourself will heal you. You are perfect no matter what your past was or what you're currently experiencing. You can't be broken. You are whole, complete, and divine. Let it all go. Feel light in your heart and mind. Claim your peace. It is a new day to celebrate yourself"

Unknown

"No matter what you›ve been through, what you›ve done, the mistakes you›ve made, the flaws you own.... you are still someone. Don't allow the weight of your past to become a heavy burden in your future"

August 18

"We are all gifted, but we have to discover the gift, uncover the gift, nurture and develop the gift and use it"

Louis Farrakhan

"Find the best version of yourself and when you do let the world know about it. It's a gift worthy of sharing"

August 19

"I'm not telling you it is going to be easy.
I'm telling you it is going to be worth it."

Arthur Williams JR

"Now tell yourself that and never give up even when the struggle seams unbearable, it too shall pass"

August 20

"You may encounter many defeats, but you must not be defeated. In fact, it may be necessary to encounter the defeats, so you can know who you are, what you can rise from, how you can still come out of it."

Maya Angelou

"Life will throw a number of obstacles in your path, accept them gracefully and skip over them with grace"

August 21

"Stop wearing your wishbone where your backbone ought to be."

Elizabeth Gilbert

"In order for your dreams to come through, you must at first wake up. Wishing is fine, but without action its merely just another tooth fairy story"

August 22

"When you are grateful, you're happy, and you become a magnet to happy people, happy situations, and magical circumstances wherever you go"

Unknown

"What you give to the universe the universe will give back to you. Give out an abundance of all things beautiful and watch your world become as beautiful as you are"

August 23

"The greatest gifts you can give your children are the roots of responsibility and the wings of independence."

#DenisWaitley

"Give your children a solid foundation to which they can build on, once they have built on those foundations give them the open space to spread their wings and soar to higher heights"

August 24

"Not everyone has access to me because I want and need peace more than attention"

Terence Wallen

"Sometimes with being popular I just want to be left alone. Everyone may know of me but not everyone knows me and I like and will keep it like that"

August 25

"Some relationships are like glass. Sometimes it is better to leave them broken than hurt yourself trying to put it back together"

Unknown

"I've had some great relationships and I've had some not so great ones. I've lost women I wished I never and I've lost women I'd never search for. In this crazy world of seeking love some relationships are best left dead rather than wasting your breath trying to give it life"

August 26

"It is difficult because I never want to be the person to cause confusion or step on toes, but I want to honor myself and I want to honor my authenticity. And if honoring my authenticity means you hate me, stone me, shoot me, crucify me, whatever, bury me an honest man."

August Alsina

"I am who i am, I'm far from perfect but my perfect imperfections makes me outstanding. If that bothers, you then take a seat with the other dick heads and fuck right off"

August 27

"You have not lived today until you have done something for someone who can never repay you"

John Bunyan

"The greatness of my character means that I constantly help, support and treat well those that can do nothing for me"

August 28

“Getting angry in a stressful situation is like trying to clean something with dirt”

Urbanky Aurel Petru

“Waste not your time and energy on things that make you waste your time and energy”

August 29

"Only through growing pains, do we learn who we truly are. When the sea is calm, one cannot judge his ability to ride the waves"

Darryl James

"We learn to weather life's storms by being in it, not by hearing about it. Life's hard experiences will soon prepare you for life's beautiful celebrations"

August 30

"It is all in the mind, change your mindset and it will change your life!"

Darryl James

"Everything starts with you, you're in control of your actions, your mind, you're thinking and your thoughts. Open your mind like a parachute and save your own life"

August 31

"Knowing tactics is important, knowing when and where to use those tactics is essential"

Darryl James

"Knowledge on its own is merely information received, the applied knowledge is what counts"

September

September 1

"Do your thing. Do it unapologetically. Don't be discouraged by criticism. Pay no mind to the fear of failure. It is far more valuable than success. Take ownership, take chances, and have fun. And no matter what, don't ever stop doing your thing."

Asher Roth

"Everyone who knows me knows that I live life to the fullest and I care zero about those who contribute zero to my existence. I will never apologise for being me, i will never compete with anyone because there is simply no competition"

September 2

"A positive attitude gives you power over your circumstances instead of your circumstances having power over you."

Joyce Meyer

"Regardless where you're from, or where you currently are, take full control of all the good things in your life, love all the good people in your life, do as many good deeds during your life and use your given powers to be the best version of your life"

September 3

"Learn to enjoy every minute of your life. Be happy. Don't wait for something outside of yourself to make you happy. Think how really precious is the time you have to spend, whether it is at work or with your family. Every minute should be enjoyed and savored."

Earl Nightingale

"One thing for sure is that times does not stop or wait for you to catch up. Once time goes you can't get it back, so value your time on earth, enjoy life, spread love, kindness, and joy wherever you go. Ensure that the quality of your life starts from within you and manifests itself in everything you do. Love the life you live and live the life you love" #MyTruth

September 4

"Remember, you are not born to stay the same. You're allowed to change, to be better, to break and become, to evolve, to shift, to learn from the breaking. If there's anything you need to do, it is to trust the process of getting to know who you're meant to"

Unknown

"None of us are the same we were years ago, how shit would that be if we didn't evolve. Life and its experiences force us to change and become better version of ourselves. Embrace all those better changes because it's those very changes that have made us into who we are today, hopefully the better person than yesterday"

September 5

"Never go to places or people that exposes your system to anything that undermines what you want to achieve, not every person or place is a conducive environment for your vision"

Unknown

"Accept that not everyone who smiles with you really likes you and that everyone that turns up their nose at you is your enemy. There are wolves in sheep's clothing and sheep parading as wolves. It's up to you to use your deep inner spirit to sense out who is not good for before it's too late, follow your intuition and that gut feeling, its usually right. Keep your circle tight, surround yourself only where the energy is positive, remember negativity breeds negativity. Choose your people and places wisely, both have the ability to undermine your progress."

September 6

"Meditation is a process of lightening up, of trusting the basic goodness of what we have and who we are, and of realizing that any wisdom that exists, exists in what we already have. We can lead our life so as to become more awake to who we are and what we're doing rather than trying to improve or change or get rid of who wc arc or what we're doing. The key is to wake up, to become more alert, more inquisitive and curious about ourselves."

Pema Chodron

"Get out your own way and find yourself. It is this finding that will open you up to your inner spirit, soul and being. From that point you will soon realise how great and powerful you really are"

September 7

"Anything that's human is mentionable, and anything that is mentionable can be more manageable. When we can talk about our feelings, they become less overwhelming, less upsetting, and less scary."

Fred Rogers

"Getting things out your system by talking to someone is a good way to lessen the weight and burden of troubled feelings. However, we must be selective with whom we share our feelings with, not everyone who listens cares"

September 8

"One small crack does not mean that you are broken, it means that you were put to the test and you didn't fall apart."

Linda Poindexter

"Never give up when your down, those very hard lessons will only make you stronger. By just being here to talk about it means you did not crumble and there is hope for all things to get better. Keep the faith"

September 9

"I cannot stand the words "Get over it". All of us are under such pressure to put our problems in the past tense. Slow down. Don't allow other to hurry your healing. It is a process, one that may take years, occasionally, even a lifetime – and that's OK."

Beau Taplin

"Do things in the time that suits you. We all are different so deal with our problems differently. We can't rush our healing to fit or suit others, it's our own journey and sometimes we simply have to travel alone, in our own space, time and methods" #MyTruth

September 10

"You don't have to be positive all the time. It is perfectly okay to feel sad, angry, annoyed, frustrated, scared and anxious. Having feelings does not make you a negative person. It makes you human."

Lori Deschene

"When you are constantly trying tirelessly to make everyone around you happy it can take its toll on your emotions, especially when theirs times when you're not feeling happy yourself. Someone once said, 'Its ok to not be ok' and that's so true. Embrace the highs & lows of life"

September 11

"Out of all the things I have lost, I miss my mind the most."

Mark Twain

"Deep....I've been there, let this be a quote of the past"

September 12

"The most beautiful people we have known are those who have known defeat, known suffering, known struggle, known loss, and have found their way out of the depths. These persons have an appreciation, a sensitivity, and an understanding of life that fills them with compassion, gentleness, and a deep loving concern. Beautiful people do not just happen."

Elisabeth Kübler-Ross

"Personally I feel like any descriptions of the most beautiful people is a description of my dear mother, and if I can be described as such in half its context I'll be a very lucky man and my story will be one worth sharing hopefully inspiring others to become beautiful people too"

September 13

"Give yourself a break. Stop beating yourself up!. Everyone makes mistakes, has setbacks and failures. You don't come with a book on how to get it right all the time. You will fail sometimes, not because you planned to, but simply because you're human. Failure is a part of creating a great life."

Les Brown

"Life would be such a dull place if we hadn't made stupid mistakes and errors along the way. I recognise success because I've experienced failure"

September 14

"As you're reading this… Congratulations, you're alive. If that's not something to smile about, then I don't know what is."

Chad Sugg

"As I'm writing this, I'm happy to be alive, I'm present in all my glory, I'm contributing greatly to the universe and I'm writing my legacy as we speak, life is for living"

September 15

"It is easy to talk about what we are going to do, but it does not mean anything until we take action and make it happen. I have a friend that is an expert at this. He talks and talks, has great plans, but where he lacks is putting those plans into action - Are one of those individuals who desire to achieve something but do more talking about what you might do as opposed to actually taking action.?"

Catherine Pulsifer

"Long talking gets you nowhere, sitting on your great ideas will not impact the world but only your mind. Get those ideas out your head and make them reality"

September 16

"Are you one of those individuals who desire to achieve something but do more talking about what you might do as opposed to actually taking action?"

Catherine Pulsifer

"Don't be the one who talks the talk but can't walk the walk. No matter what it takes put those thoughts into actions. Don't be the one labelled as the one that just chats shit"

September 17

"Adapt yourself to the life you have been given; and truly love the people with whom destiny has surrounded you with"

Marcus Aurelius

"When people say I'm blessed they are usually looking at all the wrong things, my real blessings are not of the material kind but of those who surround me with love, my real ones"

September 18

"Clear your mind of can't."

Dr. Samuel Johnson

"Fill your mind with I can & I will. Start from today by saying 'I will no longer say I can't, and I will prove that I can"

September 19

"Whenever you find yourself on the side of the majority, it is time to pause and reflect."

Mark Twain

"Stay in your own lane, its less congested. It's hard to see where you're going when you're in a crowd" #MyTruth

September 20

"The days you are most uncomfortable are the days you learn the most about yourself."

Mary L. Bean

"Difficult times call for solutions. The best side of you will appear once you are out of your comfort zone"
#MyTruth

September 21

"The beginning of love is to let those we love be perfectly themselves, and not to twist them to fit our own image. Otherwise we love only the reflection of ourselves we find in them."

Thomas Merton

"Don't try and change people, its better we change ourselves and accept their differences"
#MyTruth

September 22

"Create your own visual style... let it be unique for yourself and yet identifiable for others."

Orson Welles

"When I arrive I need not be introduced, my presence alone is the introduction"
#MyTruth

September 23

"You probably wouldn't worry about what people think of you if you could know how seldom they do."

Olin Miller

"Why give your thoughts to those that don't think about you. People are too busy with their lives to be thinking about you and if they are then you need them not in your life as they are idle" #MyTruth

September 24

"About all you can do in life is be who you are. Some people will love you for you. Most will love you for what you can do for them, and some won't like you at all."

Rita Mae Brown

"It is what it is, be yourself, let them be themselves. Love who loves you and ignore those that don't. Sleep well at night and waking up as you again" #MyTruth

September 25

"Learn everything you can, anytime you can, from anyone you can; there will always come a time when you will be grateful you did."

Sarah Caldwell

"Everyone can teach you something, we can learn from others daily, be it good or bad, Lessons learnt are valuable tools for the rest of your life" #MyTruth

September 26

"Forever tilting my crown for my real ones, we not denying our greatness, others are uncomfortable with it thou"

Terence Wallen

"I am a King, my crown changes according to my mood and even my outfit at times, what does not ever change is that I am King and will always be regardless if my crown is on my head or beside me"
#MyTruth

September 27

"Sometimes happiness looks like staying home, minding your business, telling people NO, and doing you."

Myleik Teele

"Don't overthink everything, just breathe and think you. Forget everyone else for a moment, they can wait. At this point nothing or no one is more important than you, so look in the mirror, big smiles, embrace the present and recognise this is what happiness looks like"
#MyTruth

September 28

"So many people walk around with a meaningless life. They seem half-asleep, even when they're busy doing things they think are important. This is because they're chasing the wrong things. The way you get meaning into your life is to devote yourself to loving others, devote yourself to your community around you, and devote yourself to creating something that gives you purpose and meaning"

Mitch Albom

"I never made it about me and that's why it seemed so easy. I totally dedicated my existence to making others happy and leaving a legacy other can build on. You will be so surprised what you can achieve when your humble and who gets the credit means nothing to do. Keep doing stuff with meaning and see how meaningful your whole life becomes" #MyTruth

September 29

"Happiness is the consequence of personal effort.
You fight for it, strive for it, insist upon it, & even travel around the world looking for it. And once you have achieved a state of happiness never become lax about maintaining it."

Elizabeth Gilbert

"Make it your personal quest to be nothing but happy, do what it takes, be around who can help you achieve it, go where happiness is the order of the day. Surround yourself only with positive people, positive vibes and positive energy. It must be your doing, you must want it as much as you don't want to be sad, and once you get that feeling, lock it away, protect it, keep it safe, treasure it and maintain it for ever, for now it's yours and you sure hell didn't work so hard getting it to lose it"

September 30

"If the whole world was blind, how many people would you impress? "

Boonaa Mohammed

"Your energy introduces you before you even speak, have a positive energy, it will warm the room and warm those in it"

October

October 1

"I'm busy; but not in the way most people accept. I'm busy calming my fear and finding my courage. I'm busy listening to my kids. I'm busy getting in touch with what is real. I'm busy growing things and connecting with the natural world. I'm busy questioning my answers. I'm busy being present in my life."

Brooke Hampton

"Appreciating time and using it the best way I can is the one of the best decisions I could have ever made. What I thought I was doing previously only amounted to me wasting valuable time, now I'm doing what I should have been doing i understand the real value of time"

October 2

"If you are humble nothing will touch you, neither praise nor disgrace, because you know what you are."

Mother Teresa

"Being humble is less about self and more about what we can add to the lives of others, never forget where you're coming from, do what you can to help others, maintain a humble presence no matter how high you get"

October 3

"Be grateful for what you have while working hard for what you want"

Unknown

"Don't get complacent, don't get too comfortable, appreciate all the things you have now, enjoy them now, never take your eyes off the prize, keep on keeping on"

October 4

"Never be bullied into silence, never allow yourself to be made a victim. Accept no one's definition of your life, define yourself"

Robert Frost

"No one knows you better than yourself, never allow anyone dictate to you who you are, you are you for a reason"

October 5

"Sometimes you have to blame yourself for shit you go through because you knew better"

Unknown

"Love has a way of making you blind to the obvious, even when you know its unhealthy, you remain in the unhealthy situation because you hoping that the situation will change, seldom does it. Only when your free from it will you realise how some of your pains was self-inflicted"

October 6

"If you don't heal what hurt you, you'll bleed on people who didn't cut you"

Unknown

"It's so easy to vent your anger and frustrations on those who didn't cause it. Don't risk damaging friendships and relationships because your too damaged to recognise who damaged you"

October 7

"A friend who understands your tears is much more valuable than a lot of friends who only know your smile"

Unknown

"People will surround you when you're at your best and ignore you at your worst. Know these people and separate them from early. Hang on to those real friends who stand by you regardless if your winning or not"

October 8

"Your talent is God's gift to you. What you do with it is your gift back to God."

Leo Buscaglia

"Wasted talent is a sin, and thou shall not sin. Show the almighty gratitude for giving you life, repay the life with a purpose"

October 9

"To live you must experiment, to experiment you must have confidence, to have confidence you must be loved, to be loved you must love"

Unknown

"What you put out you will receive in abundance, what you put out into the universe the universe will give you back, speak it into existence and watch it manifest"

October 10

"Let it go, it is not worth the worrrying, it is not worth fighting for. It is hurting you and breaking you, let it go. Move on and be happy."

Unknown

"Get rid of anything or anyone that does not increase you or helps you to grow. If they have exhausted their stay, then say goodbye and close the door of your life on them. If they are not there to build you then they are there to crush you. You recognise they are not worth it by firstly recognising that you are"

October 11

"The best relationships are not just about the good times you share, they're also about the obstacles you go through together, and the fact that you still say I love you in the end. And loving someone isn't just about saying it every day, it is showing it every day in every way"

Unknown

"My mum used to always say ‹words is wind' and at times you just need to feel that beautiful breeze, but with that you also need to see actions to back those words because 'actions speak louder than words'. So maintain a strong, healthy relationship by practicing what you preach"

October 12

"I've learned that fear limits you and your vision. The journey is valuable, but believing in your talents, your abilities, and your self-worth can empower you to walk down an even brighter path. Transforming fear into freedom – how great is that?"

Soledad O'Brien

"What a great feeling it is to have no fear, most of our problems, delays, shortfalls sit on the back of fear. Remove fear and watch yourself blossom into all things great and beautiful. Freedom is certainly the ultimate luxury; this can only be achieved if you remove the shackles of fear"

October 13

"Live the Life of Your Dreams: Be brave enough to live the life of your dreams according to your vision and purpose instead of the expectations and opinions of others."

Roy T Bennett

"Fu*k what others say or do; they will always have something to say. Its your life, live it how you please and to please only you"

October 14

"If you knew how hard it was, and how long it took, to rebuild my little universe of peace and happiness then you would understand why I'm so picky about who I allow in my life."

Unknown

"People tend to only see the result but never the journey, and sometimes that's ok because I didn't want them to see the journey anyway. However, when they appear only at the end to disturb what I've built then we have a problem. I choose who I choose in my life because I prefer peace, love and harmony over their false attention and ulterior motives wrapped up in 'Friendship aka 'Frenemies"

October 15

"This often offends people when I say this but I don't care. My mental health is a priority over any friendship or relationship. I will lose anyone and anything before i lose my mind"

Unknown

"Happy to drop you like a bad habit if you mess with my state of mind, you will stay around me with your fucked up, negative, toxic, poisonous and dirt like mind and expect to be entertained. My mind only has the capacity for good and positivity"

October 16

"One of the most toxic things I've ever done is ignore the bad in someone because I love them"

Unknown

"I kept thinking they would change, they would come better, it was just a phase, it too shall pass... but boy was I wrong. I simply had to accept that they are no good for me, I was good for them, I loved them but they didn't love themselves so they would have no real chance in loving me"

October 17

"I used to think the worst thing in life was to end up all alone, it is not. The worst thing in life is to end up with people who make you feel all alone."

Robin Williams

"Have you ever chosen to be with someone but both physically and mentally they are just not there? Well i have. I may as well had stayed single, the title meant nothing, that too stood alone"

October 18

"Don't dwell on unkind things. Stop seeking out the storms. Even if you are not happy, put a smile on your face. 'Accentuate the positive.' Look a little deeper for the good. Go forward in life with great and strong purpose in your heart. Love life."

Gordon B. Hinckley

"We mustn't allow ourselves to give too much time and energy to the things that upset our spirit. Stay in control of your mind, accelerate to happiness as soon as you can. Think of positive things, have positive affirmations at hand, look in the mirror and smile, do whatever it takes to harness good energy and watch your love of life shine"

October 19

"It is comforting to be liked, and to be accepted by others but it is a trap. Pleasing others means you have to conform to their expectations. There is no room for conformity in success. Make sure you want to succeed more than you want acceptance of others."

Unknown

"The acceptance from others can and will only come from the real ones, those who accept you for you. Your real ones will remain regardless if your successful or not"

October 20

"Success comes to those who don't waste their time complaining. Whenever you find yourself complaining, immediately switch gears & focus on being thankful. Gratitude has a great power. It sends us more of what we are thankful for"

IMQ

"I have no time to be complaining about what hasn't worked as I'm too busy focusing on all the things that have worked. I waste not my time thinking about all the things I don›t have but instead show gratitude for all the things I do have"

October 21

"In the book of life, the answers aren't in the back."

Charles M Schulz

"Life in all its glory and complications must be lived in order to understand it"

October 22

"It is probably my job to tell you life isn't fair, but I figure you already know that. So instead, I'll tell you that hope is precious, and you're right not to give up."

C.J. Redwine

"When I say something it's because I already know it, but when I listen to someone there's a greater possibility than ill learn something. Speak only the positives because to those my ears are tuned»

October 23

"Don't be afraid to start over again. This time you are not starting from scratch, you are starting from experience"

Unknown

"The lessons learnt on any journey will equipped you for the next stage, pick the sense from the nonsense, the good from the 'good riddance' and embrace the welcomed loss of departure. The best is yet to come"

October 24

"Some people have so little going on in their lives, they would rather discuss yours. Remember, people who try to bring you down are already below you. People only rain on your parade because they're jealous of your sun and tired of their shade."

Unknown

"The world is full of spineless individuals, actually let us bring it closer to home, your community, your associates, even some family members fit into this category. Remember bad mind does not discriminate in whose head & heart it occupies as long as the notion of negativity, jealousy and hatred exists. Let them live their empty lives trying to fill it with bringing you down, this we know will never be accomplished, so leave them always empty whilst you remain full"

October 25

"I am learning all the time. The tombstone shall be my diploma"

Eartha Kitt

"I will never stop learning because I›ve learnt that this life never stops teaching. Once I leave this earth I will have graduated with the highest honours knowing I was a good student. Then onto my next lessons wherever my soul takes me"

October 26

"It is time for me to stop being so afraid, to let go of the past. What happened, happened. It does not matter how many times I go over it in my head, think about what I should've done. It is too late. I can't change the past, but I can better shape my future."

Unknown

"It's hard to not think back and replay certain situations in my mind, I know I can›t change the past but that does not at times send a sense of uncontrollable guilt over me. The journey is one I believed I could see no happy ending, however my faith, my real ones and the grace of the almighty made me see the light at the end of the tunnel. Now my whole future is bright and those around me"

October 27

"There comes a time in your life, when you walk away from all the drama and people who create it. Forget the bad and focus on the good. Life is too short to be anything but happy. Falling down is a part of life, getting back up is living."

José N. Harris

"You know when you've had enough of the pointless wrong energies coming from pointless wrong people. Don't waste another minute of your precious life on things or people that don't increase you. You have so much to offer, so regardless of the journey don't give up"

October 28

"Never underestimate the power of dreams and the influence of the human spirit. We are all the same in this notion: The potential for greatness lives within each of us."

Wilma Rudolph

"I said I was great way before I knew I was. All too often we underestimate our own greatness, there is no time like the present to do all things possible with the greatness we have within"

October 29

"Even if you cannot change all the people around you, you can change the people you choose to be around. Life is too short to waste your time on people who don't respect, appreciate, & value you. Spend your life with people who make you smile, laugh, & feel loved."

Roy T. Bennet

"You are in control of your destiny, if you have an issue with clowns then don't visit the circus. Surround your life solely with those who add something special to your life"
#MyTruth

October 30

"Sometimes when you go through things, you bottle them up inside and try to act like everything is fine. Because you want to forget they ever happened. But you have to trust me when I say that does not work. In order for you to move on, you have to let them out."

Gwen Cole

"Anything that does not agree with the body will want to or need to come out, let it out, don›t allow it to remain and fester to the point that it damages you internally. The inner workings of your mind, body and soul needs to rid itself of anything toxic. Let it go, let it be free and in return you free yourself."

November

November 1

"I believe that everything happens for a reason. People change so that you can learn to let go, things go wrong so that you appreciate them when they're right, and sometimes good things fall apart so better things can fall together."

Marilyn Monroe

"Everything is already written. The good, the bad, the indifference. Take it in your stride, either you win, or you learn but you never lose"

November 2

"Sometimes it is better to keep silent than to tell others how you feel because it hurts knowing they can hear you, but not understand you."

Unknown

"Some things are best kept to yourself. Not everyone you speak to is really listening, they are hearing but they aren't listening and there's a big difference. Stop mid flow and ask them what you said, see what happens"

November 3

"A good leader inspires people to have confidence in the leader, a great leader inspires people to have confidence in themselves"

Unknown

"The art of leadership is not that I create and accumulate followers but that I can help to encourage others to embrace the leadership that already exists within themselves."

November 4

"Stop giving other people the power to control your happiness, your mind, and your life. If you don't take control of yourself and your own life, someone else is bound to try."

Roy T. Bennett

"Any chance a vulture gets it will swoop down and take its prey. Protect yourself at all costs from people and places that are only determined to see you fail. Happiness is yours, don't let it be taken from you"

November 5

"Don't rely on someone else for your happiness and self-worth. Only you can be responsible for that. Accept who you are – completely; the good and the bad – and make changes as you see fit – not because you think someone else wants you to be different."

Stacey Charter

"Being myself is much easier than being the fake someone else. It is so much easier being the happy me, the funny me, the deep me, the thoughtful me, the generous me, the hard working me and the non-serious me, than trying to remember who the someone else I'm trying to be. Be yourself, regardless what that looks like, its so much easier"

November 6

"Bad things do happen; how I respond to them defines my character & the quality of my life. I can choose to sit in perpetual sadness, immobilized by the gravity of my loss, or I can choose to rise from the pain & treasure the most precious gift I have-life itself."

Walter Anderson

"I'm here to tell the story, so I wasn't defeated. That within itself is the biggest gift I can have, so with that in mind I love life, show gratitude for life and live life to the best i can"

November 7

"Dear self,
Sorry for putting pressure on you.
Sorry for doubting you sometimes.
Sorry for being so hard on you lately.
Sorry for worrying so much about
what the future holds.
This time around, i will focus on you
and will love everything about you."

Unknown

"Dear Self
Thank you for speaking to me. I love me more now than ever"
Love
Me x
#MyTruth

November 8

"Learn to detach yourself. From things, events and basically anything that robs you of your peace of mind. Most things worldly fit into this category. Remember, you don't need to understand why everything happened the way it did. Let it go and let the Almighty take over!"

Mufti Menk

"Rid yourself of the BS that surrounds it. It will remain if you allow it too. Not everything will be understood but that is ok, focus on the things you do understand and those who understand you"

November 9

"May your day be filled with good thoughts, kind people and happy moments."

Anonymous

"Hence my circle is what it is, no space for waste"

November 10

"Sometimes, people will have a problem with you and spread misinformation & lies so others have a problem with you too. People that seek to destroy your character are only doing it because something about your character is destroying their inner peace. It is never personal."

from Wordstionary

"Let haters hate, they'll always find a problem. What you will find is those that dislike you really don't love themselves"

November 11

"Too many people are completely broke because their Instagram lifestyle is too expensive maintain. Forget "Fake it 'till you make it", how about "save it 'till you make it"? You HAVE TO care more about how you feel in real life, than how total strangers feel about you online!"

Steven Bartlett

"Social media can fool you and others into believing things that really exist. With the fact that nearly every aspect of people's lives is on show it would seem some people are more focused on looking successful than they are being" successful"

November 12

"Appreciate those who love you.
Help those who need you.
Forgive those who hurt you.
Forget those who leave you."

Unknown

"Love, Help, Forgive and Forget....what a great way to live. Life is quite simple, we need not" complicate things"

November 13

"Expect obstacles and face them head-on. They are going to come up, so the way you handle them is what makes all the difference."

Lance Dale

"It is what it is, everything will not be perfect, how we handle these imperfections ensuring we are not absorbed by them will make the world of difference in how we live our lives"

November 14

"But how could you live and have no story to tell?"

Fyodor Dostoyevsky

"Tu raaaas, how could you? Every single day I am writing my legacy so I am determined to make it a good one, and someone somewhere will be able to relate"

November 15

"If you are facing a new challenge or being asked to do something that you have never done before don't be afraid to step out. You have more capability than you think you do but you will never see it unless you place a demand on yourself for more."

Joyce Meyer

"If you never try or never take risks you will never know what the outcome will be. You can't grow if you remain in your comfort zone, being uncomfortable for a while is not such a bad thing if you're learning to adapt to change, step out with faith, fear has no footing on this journey"

November 16

"Life is meant to be joyful, fun, adventurous, meaningful and exciting. Having people you cherish come along for the ride is truly a blessing. Cultivating and maintaining these meaningful relationships is such an important part of life."

Anil Sinha

"It is, it is... and I make sure of it every day I wake up and I'm gifted with another chance at life. Not only is it amazing for me but also everyone in my circle that's truly amazing too. When I win, they win too, as I am nothing without those who believed in me when I didn't believe in myself"

November 17

"When we least expect it, life sets us a challenge to test our courage and willingness to change; at such a moment, there is no point in pretending that nothing has happened or in saying that we are not yet ready. The challenge will not wait. Life does not look back."

Paulo Coelho

"Sometime opportunities only knock once, sometimes you get once chance and that's it. So, don›t take for granted any opportunity to grow. The world will go on without you, so either you're on it or you'll be left behind"

November 18

"A bird sitting on a tree is never afraid of the branch breaking, because her trust is not on the branch but on it is own wings. Always believe in yourself."

Charlie Wardle

"You know you best and you are totally aware of your capabilities, so trust you and what you can achieve with being capable. Fear not what you know can't break you and focus solely on what will make you"

November 19

"The greatest wealth you could possibly possess is between your ears. We've moved from the agricultural age through the industrial age to the information age. The primary source of value today isn't labor, land or hard assets, but knowledge, information, and ideas."

via Poweropedia1

"The value of information is underrated. It is one of the most valuable assets of this day and age, everything else can hold you short term but access to information will set you up successfully long term....plus once you have the knowledge & information it can't be taken from you, now that's a long term asset"

November 20

"Time is more valuable than money. You can get more money, but you cannot get more time."

Jim Rohn

"I realised this quite sometime ago. Where as I could always make money I couldn't extend what is 24hrs, the same 24hrs we all have. Time simply does not stop, it's us that stops"

November 21

"Never stand begging for that which you have the power to earn."

Miguel de Cervantes

"You will appreciate more for what you've worked and grafted for, than you will for what is simply given to you. Don't underestimate your abilities to earn"

November 22

"It happens to everyone as they grow up. You find out who you are and what you want, and then you realize that people you've known forever don't see things the way you do. So you keep the wonderful memories, but find yourself moving on."

Nicholas Sparks

"I will leave you behind on a whim if you fail to level up. I cannot stay with you if your static and not growing. Yes, we grew together, yes, we have an history but that don't mean i owe you to remain, i am not a statue"

November 23

"If you have not read any books in 2020, you're a functioning illiterate"

Terence Wallen

"Your excluded cos your reading this, now go and order my other titles"

November 24

"A man's a man,
But when you see a king, you see the work of many thousand men"

George Eliot

"Amen. When you see us Kings you also see the great Kings that came before us and paved the way for our existence. So, as you watch us grow our kingdoms, you're also watching the outcomes of our teachers practically and spiritually"

November 25

"I am the wolf. I will be the one standing guard while my friends and family sleep at night"

Unknown

"I will forever protect my loved ones, just as they have protected me in times of darkness"

November 26

"I can be: Cold as ice. Evil as hell. Or loyal like a soldier. It all depends on you"

Unknown

"I act accordingly to how you treat me. The choice is yours as to which me you will get, choose wisely"

November 27

"Your BIGGEST supporter is a stranger and your BIGGEST hater is someone you know well"

Heath Ledger.

"Yes I said it and you now thinking and looking around you, well so you should. Not everyone who congratulates you means it or means you well, and not everyone who hasn't approached you but admires you from a distance is against you."

November 28

"Really it comes down to your philosophy. Do you want to play it safe and be good or do you want to take a chance and be great"

Jimmie Johnson

"I choose great every day. Playing it safe, not taking risks, missing opportunities would leave me average. Average is not the place for me, I aspire only towards greatness"

November 29

"Never pick a fight with an ugly person, they've got nothing to lose"

Robin Williams

"When they struggle to join you, they will then try to beat you. Don't stoop to their level, that's what they want, they want you to be the same as them but you're not. Your above them hence they trying to drag you down. Only you lose because they had nothing in the first place"

November 30

"If we stand tall, it is because we stand on the shoulders of those who came before us."

African proverb.

"That makes me just under 12ft tall, as its the shoulders of my beloved late brother that held me up to the heights I have now reached" R.I.E.P Sted. Find that shoulder you can stand on and make them proud as you attain higher heights"

*Show gratitude and respect to those who through the struggle and the battles paved the way for us that we can now proudly take on the new challenges to make easier the journey for the generations to follow"

#MyTruth

December

December 1

"The greatest challenge in life is to be our own person and accept that being different is a blessing and not a curse. A person who knows who they are lives a simple life by eliminating anything that does not align with their overriding purpose and values."

Kilroy J. Oldster

"Be who you are, they will either love you or they won't, but the real ones will love you regardless. Biggest mistake one can make is trying to please everyone, don't even try, use the energy and do what's pleasing to yourself"

December 2

"Caring for your body, mind, and spirit is your greatest and grandest responsibility. It is about listening to the needs of your soul and then honoring them."

Kristi Ling

"The best conversations you have will be the ones you have with yourself, take time to listen to you. The voice in your head, speaks to you from a deeper place, you must listen"

December 3

"Humility will open more doors than arrogance ever will."

Zig Ziglar

"The humble man is winning every time. Arrogance is just the burden we sometimes have to go through during the battle, but we already knew who would win before the battle even begun"

December 4

"A difficult life spent in hard-work, perseverance, and courage will pave the way for a life of true greatness."

Avijeet Das

"I sacrificed a few years doing the things I had to do, so I can now spend the rest of my life doing the things I want to do. Make the sacrifices from early, so later in life you can enjoy them. If you waiting for the right time you'll never be ready, the right time is now, start now"

December 5

"Fall in love with taking care of yourself.
Fall in love with the path of deep healing.
Fall in love with becoming the best version of yourself but with patience,
with compassion and respect to your own journey"

S. Mcnutt

"Love yourself the way you love others, care for yourself the way you care for others, speak positively of yourself as how you speak of others, be the best you and love yourself for it. As a matter of fact, ask yourself out, say Yes and take yourself out on a date and treat yourself how you know you deserve to be treated"

December 6

"The best feeling is when someone appreciates everything about you that someone else took for granted"

Unknown

"Bitches be hurting now and wanting what they once discarded. One woman's trash is another woman's treasure.... look at me know and look at you now, only one of us is truly happy.....me!"

December 7

"They would have treated you better if they knew who you were about to become"

Unknown

"Haters, those who watch you with envy in their eyes, who say hello but speak bad of you in their minds, who discuss you as you leave the room. Now they want to run behind you and jump on your success train? Hell no, too little too late. Keep the same energy you had when you thought I'd amount to nothing"

December 8

"To be rejected by someone does not mean you should also reject yourself or that you should think of yourself as a lesser person. It does not mean that nobody will ever love you anymore. Remember one person's opinion does not symbolize the opinion of the whole world"

Jocelyn Soriano

"There is someone for everyone in this world, and just because someone does not want you or appreciate you it does not make you a bad person.....actually it is a blessing in disguise and now your free to be loved by someone who really knows when they have found the right person"

December 9

"Leaders become great, not because of their power, but because of their ability to empower others."

John C. Maxwell

"Real leaders are only concerned in developing leaders, not recruiting followers"

December 10

"Confidence isn't walking into a room thinking you're better than everyone, it is walking in and not having to compare yourself to anyone at all"

Unknown

"Doors open...Head high, shoulders back, the energy has just gone up, the aura has magnified, my presence is felt, I've not yet said a word…I have arrived"

December 11

"A good father is one of the most unsung, unpraised, unnoticed, and yet one of the most valuable assets in our society."

Billy Graham

"There are so many great fathers out here who lead like Kings. Show them some love, let them know they are recognised and appreciated. For it is them that can help raise our future Kings & Queens and change a whole generation of thinking and being"

December 12

"I believe you have the ability to light up a room and make a person feel comfortable and special, plus its genuine. Not many people can be that present!"

Marlene Davis

"This was actually said to me by my dearest friend Marlene, so I shared it. One because it was such a touching compliment, she gave me and two because its testimony that her words are powerful, and we must not ever underestimate our greatness. To her it was just a message to the world it is now a quote"

December 13

"If only our eyes saw souls instead of bodies how different out ideals of beauty would be."

Lauren Jauregui

"We must aim to look deeper within ourselves and others, remaining on the surface will not give you an insight into what makes anything beautiful. Real beauty inside manifests itself on the outside, whereas beauty on the outside could be just that"

December 14

"Staying positive does not mean
you have to be happy all the time.
It means that even on the hard days
you know better ones are coming".

Unknown

"Stay positive and believe things will get better, it may not always seem that way but trust the process and look forward to looking back and remembering the days when things wasn't perfect but you persevered with your quest for happiness of which you have now reaching if you haven't already reached"

December 15

"You gain strength, courage, and confidence by every experience in which you really stop to look fear in the face. You are able to say to yourself, 'I lived through this horror. I can take the next thing that comes along."

Eleanor Roosevelt

"After what I have been through, I now feel I can take on anything. I thought I would not make it this far but my faith, strength, family & friends made me realise I was stronger than I thought. If I can survive that ordeal, then I know to accept that I am strong and will not be defeated. Don't underestimate your strength when you need it most"

December 16

"Don't join an easy crowd; you won't grow. Go where the expectations and the demands to perform are high."

Jim Rohn

"I loved sitting at the feet of the wise, sitting with the elders and learning whilst my peers engaged in extracurricular youth activities. I realised I made the right decisions then to create my own path and not follow a path I was uncertain where it would lead"

December 17

"The more you love your decisions, the less you need others to love them."

Unknown

"Rightfully so. As long as your happy with your decisions and you've done your best, to hell with what others think, it's your life not theirs, you either will live with the notion you got it right or deal with consequences you may of not, you win or you learn, either way your responsible and you have no regrets for making your own decisions"

December 18

"Loving can cost a lot but not loving always costs more, and those who fear to love often find that want of love is an emptiness that robs the joy from life"

Merle Shan

"I'm not afraid to love, I'll do it over and over until i get it totally right. I totally appreciate all the women I've loved before, time spent in love cannot be replaced so I'm grateful for every love I've had be it good or bad it's been part of my journey and part of my experiences. No regrets when it comes to being loved or giving love"

December 19

"Money can buy a house, but not a home. Money can buy a bed, but not sleep. Money can buy a clock, but not time. Money can buy a book, but not knowledge. Money can buy food, but not appetite. Money can earn a position but not respect. Money can buy blood but not health. Money can buy friends but not love. Money can buy insurance but not safety. Money is not everything in life."

Unknown

"The only real benefits of having money is the freedoms it comes with, other than that having it so overrated and I wish people would place more value on the things money can't buy. I had money, then I had more money, but I have lost what really mattered to me and that has made me feel broke. I would give up any wealth for time spent with my loved ones lost & present"

December 20

"Life is not about being rich, popular, highly educated, or even being perfect. It is about being real, being humble, and being kind."

Unknown

"If making money is your only ambition then you may obtain wealth but lose your soul. It is better to be loved for who you are than to be loved for what you got. Everyone I know of wealth came from humble beginnings and have remained humble with growth. The acquirements and lifestyle may change but the authenticity remains.»

December 21

"Life is not about who hurt you and broke you down. It is about who was always there and who made you smile again."

Unknown

"I really can't focus or spend time giving my energy to haters because I'm so absorbed in giving my time and energy to those I love and love me"

December 22

"Women who marry for money and Men who marry for beauty are equally robbed in the end"

Harmon Okinyo

"Either way they both can dwindle, marry because your souls and hearts meet as only, they will remain long after everything else has faded"

December 23

"Life is amazing, then it is awful. In between the amazing & awful it is ordinary. Breathe in the amazing, hold on through the awful, relax & exhale during the ordinary. That's just living heartbreaking, soul-healing, amazing, awful, ordinary life. And it is breathtakingly beautiful"

Miki McCarthy

"Even with all its craziness, life is beautiful and must be appreciated. The things that go wrong only strengthens us and lets us appreciate all the things that have and will go right. Life is for living; it is not enough to just be alive"

December 24

"Connecting with those you know love, like and appreciate you restores the spirit and gives you energy to keep moving forward in this life."

Deborah Day

'You really don't need a lot of people in your life, what you need is the right people in your life. Quality over quantity any day. My team are my biggest motivators, they do it for me and in return i do it for them"

December 25

"The very least you can do in your life is figure out what you hope for. And the most you can do is live inside that hope. Not admire it from a distance but live right in it, under its roof."

Barbara Kingsolver

"Sometimes you just must throw yourself in, sink or swim. Believe in yourself and immerse yourself into your growth as if your life depended on it. At the end of the day all you really have is you so you may as well put you first"

December 26

"Nobody wants to experience bad things. However, they happen. Don't run away from any of the decisions you have made. They are what you are today. Accept it. And the healing process will begin."

Pragya Tiwari

"We've all been there, we've all messed up and made mistakes, we are born into sin so it's going to happen. However, we must face and accept our flaws to prevent people using them against us. Have no regrets for the errors you made yesterday as they have been instrumental in who you are today...and your better than you were then"

December 27

"Why waste time proving over and over how great you are, when you could be getting better?"

Carol S Dweck

"To hell with trying to convince people your great, it will show regardless in your actions and presence. The time and energy wasted on putting it out there to gain points from people that don't really matter, you could simply be improving yourself in which case its manifestation would mean they won't be able to avoid your greatness anyway"

December 28

"If you surround yourself with the good and righteous, they can only raise you up. If you surround yourself with the others, they will drag you down into the doldrums of mediocrity, and they will keep you there, but only as long as you permit it."

Mark Glamack

"Come sit with me and my peers, its one way to guarantee positivity from the outset. If not create your own dream team and make that all you need to raise up, otherwise you will end up being surrounded by the wrong people whose only intent is to bring you down"

December 29

"The past is a place of reference, not a place of residence; the past is a place of learning, not a place of living"

Roy T Bennett

"I'm not looking back because I'm not going that way. My past helped pave my future, my future looks bright, why would I go back to the darkness. I do not live in my past; I live in the present because it is a gift"

December 30

"If you don't see it with your own eyes or hear it with your own ears, don't invent it with your small mind and share it with your big mouth"

Denise Swanson

"I can't stand people that just chat shit for the sake of having something to say. Remove anyone like this from your life and god forbid this quote is about you, in which case thanks for buying my book but you too can remove yourself"

December 31

"Those who do not move, do not notice their chains"

Rosa Luxemburg

"Let nothing hold you back, explore, travel, live, learn, do the things you only dreamt of doing, take risks, live on the edge, embrace freedom, don't let those invisible chains hold you back. You will regret all the things you wished you didn't do because you spent too much time thinking about them instead of acting on them"

Bonus Truths For Those Extra Shitty Days

"It is hard to beat a person who never gives up."

Babe Ruth

"Have defeats, but never be defeated. Let them use all their energies, time, effort, weapons, negativity, lies and bullshit to try and bring you down, it's their energy being wasted, preserve yours and remain calm and present. Knowing full well at all stages that you refuse to be defeated. Your journey continues and hell no will you stop to be part of the circus of clowns that try to distract you. Be not fooled, some will not give up and are destined to see you fail, but your desire to be great is untouchable and unbeatable. You win." #MyTruth

"Employ your time in improving yourself by other men's writings so that you shall come easily by what others have labored hard for."

Socrates

"I encourage you to explore more, read more, source more, find those gems of wisdom placed out in the universe for you to discover. So many greats before us have paved the way with an abundance of truths and affirmations that can only make the path clearer for us. You will be doing yourself an injustice if you let the work of others great writers not fuse your mind and thoughts because of ignorance. By virtue you're doing it now by reading this, so your already embracing, I'm encouraging you to do more and find the others...as I did"

"History has demonstrated that the most notable winners usually encountered heartbreaking obstacles before they triumphed. They won because they refused to become discouraged by their defeats."

Bertie Charles Forbes

"We've all been there, that place that has left us empty and deflated. Those times when we feel like just throwing in the towel because at that point, we just don't see no light at the end of the tunnel. When we repeatedly try and feel like we simply not getting nowhere, and nothing seems to be going right. What we missed was that was all part of your journey, the downs so you can show strength on the ups, the setbacks so you can ready yourself for the comebacks, the defeats so you can shine on the wins. No matter what life throws at you, just know that this too will pass and believe things will get better. You are here for a purpose and that purpose is not to be defeated"

"Whatever your storybook carries within its pages, own it with love, courage and compassion. Remember that you can change your story at any time- nothing is fixed, and we all have free will. Never seek to love someone else's journey. We all have our own paths."

Christine Evangelou

"Make every day yours, it can't be someone else's because we all walk different paths. Your story is unique to you and someone somewhere loves it and is encouraged by it. Every day of your life you are writing your legacy, make it a good one, joyful, purposeful and rememberable. With every new day comes a new chapter, be the author of your destiny"

"Life is more than work. Life is also about balance. In order to have balance, we must do more than work. What about fun? How about rest? Work is necessary but it is not the only thing required to get ahead"

Iyanla Vanzant

"We can't simply be alive to pay bills and then die, what a waste of this great gift called life. Life itself must be lived and to its fullest as once it has gone its gone. Society has forced us into working long hours to afford the things society say we must have, we must know the difference between want and need, only then will we truly prioritise our way of living. Take time out to love yourself, love the life you love, be grateful for what you have, appreciate those good around you and know that work in isolation will only drive you into the ground and its all the other things that will lift you up"

Acknowledgements

My sincerest, deepest, heartfelt appreciation to my daughter Shelika for her committed contribution to this book. The long days, the late nights, the stressful abundance of emails from me and the publisher, the changes that I changed again and then changed again, the dedicated attempts to juggle motherhood and stay on top of my projects, your patience, your professionalism, your quest for greatness keeps me inspired. I'm truly indebted to you. Thank you for being you and forever allowing me to be me.

I wouldn't be the adored 'Pop-Pop' if I didn't acknowledge my grandson Kareem, thank you for running riot when we needed peace and quiet, thank you for nearly losing the whole transcript with one push of the laptop of the bed, throwing the whole project into panic unsure if everything was backed up, thank you for playing hide & seek with yourself (because I was not coming to find you) which gave us the peace we needed to get stuff done and thank you for giving me a fresh lease on life being a Grandad and a bloody cool one at that.

My Mother, my forever driver, my biggest inspiration. How proud you were when I put out my 1st book, now I'm doing it again and I'll continue to make you proud. I love the way when I told you my book will be in Asda you said "Ok that's good, while you there can you grab me some Oranges, Milk and Honey lolol, classic humbled response, I can't thank you enough for my very existence. "All I am and all I hope to be, I owe to you for the love you gave to me" - (Taken from I.O.U by Gregory Isaacs). Mum I love you.

My late beloved brother Sted, I'll keep pressing on with your guidance, stay with me, I can't and don't ever want to do it alone, we in this together and all my achievements will also be yours.

My Children, I'm nothing without you. Thank you for the continued show of love and proudness. Even when I get it wrong, even with the flaws that come with being human and being a father, even when I sacrifice fatherhood to fulfil my dreams and aspirations you all still find it in your hearts to show love. The only other words that touch my every being other than MyTruth is hearing you guys say MyDad, I love you all x

Sydney Bartley my mentor, my big brother, my best friend, my guide and now my quest to see him good as a way of saying thank you. Thank you for answering every question I randomly ask, every document I need looking over, every idea I have but need to run by you to ensure I'm making sense. Sometimes you perhaps don't get the credit you deserve from countless individuals whose lives you've changed for greatness; I'm truly indebted to you. To think you were consistent with Sted and now just as consistent or even more with me, I'm truly grateful. The one truth I need from you.... do you want your Bentley in Black or White?

My Team, My People, My Family...what a journey, so much greatness in one small group, the support, the motivation, the encouragement, the corrections, the drawing me back in when I forget myself, the love, the security, and the togetherness is all I need (oh and the food, don't forget my food). I love you guys. No squares in my circle

To the AMAZING publishing company DMJ Publishing, what a team, what a belief in me. Thank you for extending my deadlines and meeting my demands lol. Looking forward to a fruitful continued relationship, I'll sign on that dotted line again. Only if you ensure I'm your priority client though lol #MyTruth

To everyone who has contributed to the chapters of my life, you have all played a major part, be it good or bad, big, or small, I've learnt regardless and for that I'm truly grateful.

Last but certainly not least, The Almighty, who has guided me through every emotion and was always present when I needed someone to talk to. Thanks for listening and answers my prayers. My imperfections and failures are as much a blessing from God as my successes and my talents and I lay them both at his feet, truly grateful, truly humbled.

#MyTruth

• Contributions

Heartfelt appreciation and humble recognition is given to all the authors credited and those unknown for sharing their work with the world, being the voice of reason, the inspiration needed, the words of wisdom counted on, the opening of minds, body, and spirit. Thank you for being my personal motivator and allowing me to expand and give my personal take on your contributions to life itself.

• #MyTruth

www.ingramcontent.com/pod-product-compliance
Lightning Source LLC
LaVergne TN
LVHW010557100826
845148LV00014B/2749

* 9 7 8 1 8 3 8 1 8 8 4 7 4 *